Strategies and Consequences:
Managing the Costs in Higher Education

by John S. Waggaman

ASHE-ERIC Higher Education Report No. 8, 1991

Prepared by

Clearinghouse on Higher Education
The George Washington University

In cooperation with

Association for the Study
of Higher Education

Published by

School of Education and Human Development
The George Washington University

Jonathan D. Fife, Series Editor

Cite as

Waggaman, John S. 1991. *Strategies and Consequences: Managing the Costs in Higher Education.* ASHE-ERIC Higher Education Report No. 8. Washington, D.C.: The George Washington University, School of Education and Human Development.

Library of Congress Catalog Card Number 92-81698
ISSN 0884-0040
ISBN 1-878380-13-3

Managing Editor: Bryan Hollister
Manuscript Editor: Alexandra Rockey
Cover design by Michael David Brown, Rockville, Maryland

The ERIC Clearinghouse on Higher Education invites individuals to submit proposals for writing monographs for the *ASHE-ERIC Higher Education Report* series. Proposals must include:
1. A detailed manuscript proposal of not more than five pages.
2. A chapter-by-chapter outline.
3. A 75-word summary to be used by several review committees for the initial screening and rating of each proposal.
4. A vita and a writing sample.

ERIC **Clearinghouse on Higher Education**
School of Education and Human Development
The George Washington University
One Dupont Circle, Suite 630
Washington, DC 20036-1183

This publication was prepared partially with funding from the Office of Educational Research and Improvement, U.S. Department of Education, under contract no. ED RI-88-062014. The opinions expressed in this report do not necessarily reflect the positions or policies of OERI or the Department.

EXECUTIVE SUMMARY

The need for better management of higher education's resources is a theme of great urgency as 40 states plan or actually cut appropriations to higher education and other public
services. The 1987 hearings in Congress about higher education costs and the several reports which have appeared in
the past 30 months provide data and information about cost
trends, tuition increases, and explanations for the changes.

The breadth of this topic has required a wide-ranging survey of the professional literature covering several decades,
for many of these problems have been encountered before,
for example, the late 1960s. The topic cuts across many
aspects of higher education: general revenues, the relationship
of costs to tuition increases, faculty salaries and work load,
research expenses, administrative costs, and other related
subjects. Management actions, practices, and strategies in both
private and public colleges and universities are discussed;
the short- and long-range responses to financial emergencies
are described.

The persistent theme is that analysis, planning, budgeting,
and managing can prepare us for an uncertain financial future.
We can avoid many of the more damaging pitfalls if we know
the secondary consequences of the more typical ad hoc decisions made when financial difficulties arrive.

What Are the Rising Costs and Changing Revenues?
Although tuition continues to increase, it has been rising at
a decreasing rate of growth since its peak in 1981 (Frances
1990). Rising costs are partly responsible for tuition increases
as well as spending pressures and revenue shortfalls, according to Frances. Uncontrollable costs come from the marketplace and government mandates; spending pressures emerge
from salary and fringe-benefit costs.

It still is true that faculty salaries have not increased suf-
ficiently to compensate for the losses during the runaway
inflation of the 1970s (Hauptman 1990). The 1990-1992 recession promises to make this problem worse. The anticipation
of the enrollment decline in the number of high school graduates in the 1990s has led private institutions to spend funds
to make campuses more attractive, add programs, and carry
out full-fledged marketing campaigns for new students. Administrative costs have risen as much as two percentage points
over the past decade, but the causes are not clear. The rise
could be attributed to more student services and programs

to meet governmental social policy and health and safety requirements, and the expanding use of computers in all kinds of administrative functions (Chaney and Farris 1990). The 1990 Chaney and Farris survey of financial officers indicated a majority thought that the addition of computers and the upgrading of computer facilities (72 percent) were very important causes in the 1980s. Rising insurance costs were selected by 71 percent of the officers as a major cost pressure.

Revenue shortfalls occur in two ways: a relative decline in the rate of growth so that inflation or other factors rise faster than revenues or an actual decrease in funding occurs. Endowment earnings for 1989-90 were at their lowest in a decade. By early 1992, it appeared that 22 states had cut 1992 appropriations to higher education; more are expected. The unwillingness of Congress to fully fund student aid up to the amounts it had authorized or to keep aid level with inflation makes it harder for students to obtain adequate funding at even low-cost public institutions.

However, the federal government still funds or underwrites almost three-fourths of student aid awarded in the United States. Unfortunately, that rate is down from 83 percent in 1980-81. These declines have caused public institutions and many private ones to spend more of their unrestricted general funds for student aid—as much as 25 percent of total aid in many institutions—up from 12 percent in 1980-81 (Frances 1990).

Institutions have been making very serious commitments in support of their special responsibility to recognize talent and help it enroll in college. Institutional aid also may help recruit students to offset some of the decline in the number of high school graduates. However, funds used for one purpose (or not collected) cannot be used to enhance programs or the salaries of faculty and staff. These latter needs might translate into pressures to raise tuition further so that more funds can be obtained for educational programs or other special purposes. A conceptual explanation of the dynamics of rising costs and revenues can be found in "The Lattice and the Ratchet" and other articles published in *Policy Perspectives* (June 1990 and later) of the Pew Higher Education Research Program.

How Can We Manage and Control Costs?
The Chaney and Farris survey revealed that financial officers (81 percent) were quite confident about being able to control

expenditures. If anyone should doubt that possibility, they should recall the finding from Cheit's follow-up study in 1973. He revisited the institutions he identified in 1971 that were in financial difficulty and found they had cut annual expenditure growth from 4.0 percent to 0.5 percent, a reduction called "phenomenal" by Clark Kerr.

Today, after several potential management "revolutions" (Keller 1983; Rourke and Brooks 1966), colleges and universities have a variety of management tools available to help control costs, *once the leaders and administrators have decided to do so.* Some institutions successfully have adopted various information, analysis, and accountability methods to improve their planning and management abilities (Baldridge and Tierney 1979). However, there is no single strategy for successfully managing costs. Furthermore, the management revolutions might have been only partially successful, although the current fiscal crisis should stimulate increased interest in these tools and techniques.

There are some common themes in the reports about what could or should be part of a cost management strategy. First is to clarify the mission of the institution, then set priorities among the programs (educational, service, administrative, student, etc.). Strategic planning with a clear focus on both the external environment and internal operations is necessary to build a data base of trends and projections about revenues and costs. Break-even analyses for the various programs need to be calculated to determine which programs are financially self-supporting, those that break even, and those that require subsidies. Data from the break-even analyses, along with a thorough program review, should reveal the areas from which funds could be obtained for enhancements and new programs. Many other activities need to be considered—such as those that revolve around administrative compliance procedures—so that funding requests and accountability reports are accepted at face value. These strategies should be in place before the next financial emergency arrives. Otherwise, it's back to short-term ad hoc solutions, some undesirable secondary consequences, and then a search for better solutions, with such processes spiraling on into the future. One can't help wondering if there isn't a better way.

ADVISORY BOARD

Alberto Cabrera
Arizona State University

Jay Chronister
University of Virginia

Carol Everly Floyd
Board of Regents of the Regency Universities System
State of Illinois

Elizabeth Hawthorne
University of Toledo

L. Jackson Newell
University of Utah

Barbara Taylor
Association of Governing Boards of Universities and Colleges

CONSULTING EDITORS

A. Nancy Avakian
Metropolitan State University

Paula Y. Bagasao
University of California System

Rose R. Bell
New School for Social Research

Clifton F. Conrad
University of Wisconsin–Madison

James Cooper
FIPSE College Teaching Project

John W. Creswell
University of Nebraska-Lincoln

Donald F. Dansereau
Texas Christian University

Peter Frederick
Wabash College

Virginia N. Gordon
Ohio State University

Wesley R. Habley
American College Testing

Michael L. Hanes
West Chester University

Edward R. Hines
Illinois State University

Dianne Horgan
Memphis State University

Donald Hossler
Indiana University

John L. Howarth
Private Consultant

Joan Isenberg
George Mason University

Susan Jeffords
University of Washington

Margaret C. King
Schenectady County Community College

REVIEW PANEL

Charles Adams
University of Massachusetts-Amherst

Louis Albert
American Association for Higher Education

Richard Alfred
University of Michigan

Philip G. Altbach
State University of New York-Buffalo

Marilyn J. Amey
University of Kansas

Louis C. Attinasi, Jr.
University of Houston

Robert J. Barak
Iowa State Board of Regents

Alan Bayer
Virginia Polytechnic Institute and State University

John P. Bean
Indiana University-Bloomington

Louis W. Bender
Florida State University

John M. Braxton
Vanderbilt University

Peter McE. Buchanan
Council for Advancement and
    Support of Education

John A. Centra
Syracuse University

Arthur W. Chickering
George Mason University

Shirley M. Clark
Oregon State System of Higher Education

Darrel A. Clowes
Virginia Polytechnic Institute and State University

John W. Creswell
University of Nebraska-Lincoln

Deborah DiCroce
Piedmont Virginia Community College

CONTENTS

FOREWORD

This report is about those expenses institutions must pay in order to remain in business—those expenses that, for many institutions, exceed revenue and threaten their survival. To some administrators and even more faculty, the increases in these costs seem to be uncontrollable and in many cases unfathomable. In fact, with appropriate financial accounting and analysis, these costs are both manageable and understandable.

However, the impact of managing these costs is unique to each institution, simply because of the uniqueness of the educational vision and mission of each institution. Therefore, while this report will aid administrators and faculty in understanding the strategies and general short-term consequences of controlling costs, successful management of specific long-term effects depends on an institutionwide understanding of the important elements of its mission.

One of the most common responses when costs exceed revenues is to make cross-institution cuts in the least painful expenses. This usually means avoiding cuts in current personnel, especially tenured faculty. At first, these cost controls are seen in the reduction of travel funds or photocopying and support services. As the financial picture worsens, vacant staff and faculty positions are not filled and graduate and research assistants are not replaced. Each of these steps is taken to control costs. Yet, when they are taken without regard to the mission of the institution, there are no assurances that such short-term steps have any real power to maintain long-term control over costs.

Another way to manage the costs in higher education is not to look at specific expenses as costs, but approach costs as the result of specific activities. When expenses are seen this way, it becomes easier to look at both how well an activity fits the mission of the institution as well as at its ability to be financially justified. An activity can be very important, or unimportant, to the mission. It might be financially viable, bringing in more income than it costs, or it might have more expenses than revenue and be financially draining. With this simple structure, an activity can be classified into four categories: important to the mission and financially viable, important to the mission and financially draining, unimportant to the mission and financially viable, or unimportant to the mission and financially draining.

Without clearly understanding the mission of an activity

and how it relates to the mission of the institution, it is not possible to even begin this system of cost management. If the mission is understood, it is a relatively simple decision to eliminate those activities that are both unimportant to the mission and financially draining. The next group of activities to review—the most challenging—contains those which are important to the mission but are financially draining. When decision makers evaluate these activities against the total financial health and mission of the institution, then they truly are using a strategy to manage their costs with the long-term consequences in mind.

John S. Waggaman, associate professor and former coordinator of the Higher Education Program at Florida State University, Tallahassee, created this report in response to the urgent need for better management of higher education's resources. In the proceeding chapters, he discusses the sources of current cost and revenue problems; the relationship of costs to tuition increases; and general revenues, faculty salaries and work load, research expenses, and administrative costs. He also explores management actions, practices, and strategies in both private and public colleges and universities and points out successful responses to familiar problems.

Understanding where costs come from is a beginning step in gaining control. However, taking action to reduce costs without carefully considering what the change means to the long-term mission of the institution might be an act of controlled destruction. This report provides guidance for developing strategies to manage costs with the long-term consequences in mind. Unfortunately, this guidance will have little effect if the institutional leaders at all levels do not have the courage to carefully define the institution's mission.

Jonathan D. Fife
Series Editor, Professor of Higher Education Administration, and Director, ERIC Clearinghouse on Higher Education

ACKNOWLEDGMENTS

It is never too late to recognize two important people who shared information and insights about the field of higher education finance. M.M. Chambers was a teacher and early mentor who shared much more than his writings. It was reassuring to find a political scientist working in this field and to find a person so full of optimism for the future of higher education.

John Dale Russell taught me about the gender differences in salaries and many other issues that in 1967 had not reached the attention of most college and university administrators; today, they are front and center. I wish to honor the memory of both of these wise men.

In addition, I thank all those people in Florida and across the United States in the higher education planning and governance agencies, state government and legislatures, and in collegiate institutions who have been willing to share their knowledge and understanding about issues in higher education. Thanks to all of you, especially our doctoral graduates, who are willing to teach their former professor.

I also wish to thank the anonymous reviewers who made a number of suggestions to enhance this report.

Finally, I thank my wife and daughter for their love and kindness during the gestation and preparation of this report.

CENTRAL ISSUES OF MANAGING COSTS

This section introduces the major issues related to managing costs and describes the organization of the report. Both contemporary and historical materials are reviewed; the topics of tuition and costs, cost control, and cost studies especially are important. These introductory topics summarize the relevant literature, provide background information, and identify the perennial issues.

The basic literature that exists about cost management outlines a history of financial difficulties and a variety of studies. Many of the problems and proposed solutions have been around for a long time. A conceptual approach to this literature is that it represents the pragmatics of higher education administration; an analysis represents a study of the financial and management culture of higher education. The natural structure of financial and management issues is used throughout this report to organize and present the findings of this integrative literature review.

The need to better manage higher education's resources is a theme of great urgency. . . .

The need to understand these issues is clear. The demand for better higher education resource and cost management emerges from domestic and international pressures; the challenges are everywhere.

In the face of declining student enrollment, escalating costs, and tightening funding sources, higher education administrators recognize they must maximize revenues, efficiently use resources, and minimize costs while maintaining—or improving—the academic excellence of their institutions (Horwitz and Rolett 1991, p. 33).

The need to better manage higher education's resources is a theme of great urgency as 40 states plan or implement appropriation cuts to higher education and other public services. However, the messages of the new Cassandras of higher education management must be examined in the light of the experiences of the late 1960s, 1970s, and early 1980s (Johnstone 1990).

The criticism of college and university costs and quality might be inevitable given the contradictory positions about higher education taken by the public and by government officials. For example, some want universities to contribute more to technological development so the United States will be more competitive in world markets and to develop a highly trained work force. Concurrently, others condemn universities for the faculty teaching loads they perceive as "low." Perhaps these contradictions never can be resolved to everyone's satisfaction, but citizens and taxpayers still show great support for the overall benefits of higher education. The willingness of those with access to the resources to pay rising tuitions very clearly demonstrates this support.

One action most often recommended in the literature is that faculty, staff, and administrators should take responsibility to better manage the revenues and costs of our colleges and universities. This monograph describes a variety of practices that are widely used for this purpose; some of these practices should be fine-tuned and emulated, while others should be avoided if at all possible. As we sometimes must take the bad with the good—especially in financially difficult times—it is important to be fully aware of the secondary consequences that flow from many financial-decision alternatives.

If any single message runs through this monograph, it is that analysis, planning, budgeting, and managing can prepare us for an uncertain future. Responding in an ad hoc fashion, rather than in a planned or anticipatory manner, not only affects the quality of services offered, it also injures the morale of faculty and staff and their ability to maintain a commitment to excellence. We can do better, as many experts are wont to tell us. However, in many cases we are caught in the flood tide of external events over which we have little control. In order to cope effectively, we need to learn workable management strategies.

This report does not prescribe a recipe for solving the problems of financial management; that might never be possible given the variety of missions, programs, and emphases of America's 3,300 public and private colleges and universities. Although financial problems might appear similar among many institutions, the solutions often are shaped by local history and culture. However, it is useful to learn about the experiences of others and the recommendations made by the experts addressing these financial problems.

The first set of issues considered here focus on the relationship between tuition and costs. Because the availability of revenues determines expenditures, it is important to examine this element first. The next section will cover all of the revenue sources and their cost aspects.

Rising Tuition and Costs
Frances offers three reasons behind tuition increases in the 1980s: cost pressures, spending pressures, and revenue short-

falls (1990, p. 8). She notes uncontrollable costs whose prices are set in the marketplace (or, I would add, by government fiat); her list of cost pressures includes student shifting into higher-cost majors, the impact of new technology such as computers, socially mandated programs plus social security, and the cost of borrowing to purchase land, buildings, and equipment.

Spending pressures, according to Frances, result principally from compensating faculty and staff who consume up to 80 percent of the education budget. Pressures result when faculty members compare their salaries with the rewards offered to those in other professions, opportunities for alternative employment, and the need to attempt to restore the purchasing power of faculty salaries that was lost to the runaway salary inflation of the 1970s.

Another analyst adds that the perceived or actual decline in the number of high school graduates has driven up recruiting expenditures (Hauptman 1990). He also notes the increase of one to two percentage points in administrative costs and a matching decrease in spending for educational activities. Hauptman criticizes the 1988 Department of Education study of administrative costs by Snyder and Galambos, citing that the study authors didn't indicate the extent to which these costs increased as student services were added, compliance with new social policy rules expanded, or that no other factors that stimulated the cost increases were identified.

Both authors indicate that the revenue shortfalls of the 1980s—from both state and federal sources—led to compensatory increases in tuition even at state institutions in which tuition covers only a small share of the total cost of education. And by using a student-cost index, Frances shows that the growth of student financial aid was slower in the 1980s than was the increase in student costs, although financial aid exceeded the cost index in the 1970s. (See the reports of both Frances and Hauptman for their substantive explanations and aggregate tables of national data.)

Another way to study rising costs is to survey the chief financial officers of colleges and universities; Chaney and Farris conducted one such survey of 473 public and private colleges and universities in 1990. Officers surveyed reported that the cost and revenue factors which had the greatest impact on tuition were an increase in academic expenditures

(44 percent), an increase in operating expenditures (39 percent), state tuition policy requirements (37 percent), and a desire to improve the quality of the institution (35 percent). However, this list changes substantially when public and private institutions are grouped separately. For public institutions, the most important factors were state tuition policy requirements and a decrease in the proportion of state/local funding; these two factors rarely were cited by the private institutions. Very important factors for the private colleges were an increase in operating expenditures, increase in institutional student aid, and a decrease in the proportion of federal funding.

More than 80 percent of the financial officers rated their institution's ability to control expenditures as either excellent or good. The five expenditure categories which rose faster than inflation at their institutions during the period between 1980-81 and 1987-88 were insurance costs (71 percent), marketing and recruiting costs (58 percent), computing equipment and facilities (54 percent), administrative computing (53 percent), and the cost of complying with government regulations (53 percent).

The three categories which had the largest effect on increasing nonacademic expenditures were insurance costs (37 percent), marketing and recruiting costs (29 percent), and the costs of administrative computing (27 percent). The single category in which more officers (42 percent) said the increases were less than inflation was with regard to the salaries of part-time faculty. Another important cost factor was the renovation or expansion of facilities. Between 1980-81 and 1987-88, 72 percent cited an upgrade in computing facilities, 48 percent cited an upgrade in academic and research facilities, and 33 percent cited an upgrade in library facilities. The important conclusion here is that increases in costs—as well as stable or declining revenues—have contributed to tuition increases.

Management and Control of Costs
The Chaney and Farris survey of financial officers also requested information about controlling costs or improving management:

Of 15 actions that potentially could help to control costs (whether or not these actions were taken for that reason),

*the actions selected most often by respondents as having
a great impact were implementing institutionwide budget
cuts (28 percent), delaying or modifying new construction
(24 percent), or increasing the use of part-time faculty (21
percent). Between 42 and 62 percent of the respondents
claimed that these actions were taken at their institutions*
(pp. 23-4).

The secondary consequences of such actions are described
in later sections of this report. Two of the more surprising
findings about actions that are *not* likely to show an effect
on costs were establishing cooperative programs (41 percent)
and reorganizing the administration (25 percent).

A high percentage of the financial officers reported undertaking three action choices: improving the budgeting process
(82 percent), developing a strategic plan (78 percent), and
implementing or modifying a management information system (68 percent). These three programs are elements of the
management revolution reported by Rourke and Brooks
(1966) and Keller (1983). In all, one-third of the officials surveyed reported that these initiatives were very effective and
two-thirds indicated they were somewhat effective. Baldridge
and Tierney indicate how these initiatives can be effective
in small private colleges (1979).

A conclusion drawn from the survey of financial officers
is that they are more confident about controlling expenditures
than they are about increasing revenues. Their optimism is
contrary to the opinions cited in a critical article published
in a 1990 issue of *Change* which features the need for and
the inherent problems of cost containment. A review of the
difficulties in linking budgets and plans can be found in
Schmidtlein (1989-90). A more balanced treatment of the difficulties in managing costs can be found in chapter four of
Minimizing Costs: Institutional, State, and Federal Options
(Kirshstein et al. 1990, pp. 103-34). The concluding section
of that chapter states:

*At each level, changes have been proposed—and many
implemented—to restrain further escalation in higher education costs. However, most of these policy options come with
tradeoffs attached: costs are either transferred from one
party to another, shifted from the present to the future, or
reduced [to the detriment] of some other aspect of Amer-*

ican higher education, such as choice or quality. Reducing costs is thus far more complex than simply cutting institutional expenditures. Any efforts to cut costs must consider the diversity of American higher education, the tradeoffs which occur when costs are reduced, and the fact that Americans have high expectations for their colleges and universities (p. 134).

It is hard to disagree with those sentiments. However, it is important to note that many of the problems of managing costs have a long history.

Cost Studies of Earlier Decades
One of the earliest studies cited (Russell 1931) about costs in higher education was by Stevens and Elliott in *The Unit Costs of Higher Education* (1925). This study used as an output measure expenditures per student credit hour. Russell explains in his dissertation study that real outputs could not be known at that time, so the expenditure data would have to serve as a surrogate measure for outputs.

Data for Russell's study of efficiency in college operations was obtained from 31 colleges that were affiliated with the Methodist Episcopal Church. Russell initially focused on inefficiencies, the first of which involved teaching personnel. Measures included a teaching staff larger than necessary (a ratio of less than 20 to 1 of students to teachers); light instructional loads (less than 15 credit hours a week); small classes (less than 20 students); and inadequate provisions for supervising instruction. Many other categories and measures were used and covered all functions and activities of a typical college.

The final step involved computing expenditures per student and per functional category and then comparing the inefficient expenditures. Thus, using a standard methodology, standardized costs could be generated across 31 colleges and then compared to reveal the most efficient and least efficient colleges. Russell discussed these and related ideas in his 1954 revised edition of *The Finance of Higher Education*, which was reprinted several times—as late as 1967.

It should be obvious that many of the current problems of preparing a cost analysis of institutional resources were identified more than 60 years ago. The same questions still are being asked: How many classes comprise less than 10 students? Do faculty teach enough courses, credit hours, and undergraduate students? A review of cost studies and costing concepts from earlier years through the 1950s and 1960s can be found in Witmer's 1972 article in the *Review of Educational Research. The Sixty College Study* (liberal arts colleges), *The Council of Ten Study*, and others were reviewed.*

A large number of cost-related studies appeared in the late 1960s and early 1970s. The slowing of revenues after the doubling of college enrollments between 1960 and 1969 brought a cost-income squeeze and a critical need to curtail or control costs. One of the more sophisticated analyses of costs and expenditures used microeconomics to study the economies of scale of institutional operations—such as the shifts in cost as enrollment changes (Maynard 1971). An analysis of revenue and expenditure data for 66 small liberal arts colleges, somewhat in the Russell tradition, emphasized the link between cost analysis and planning (Meeth 1974). A list of recommendations for institutional effectiveness and an annotated bibliography were included.

A broader based study which focused on various kinds of institutions in financial difficulty was *The New Depression in Higher Education* (Cheit 1971). Of the 41 institutions sampled, 12 were not experiencing difficulty. The financial characteristics of the untroubled colleges revealed they usually had good relations on campus and in town, smaller student-aid expenditures, a more controlled rate of program growth, lower average compensation, administrators who believed that their institutions were quite efficient, less difficulties when federal support declined because they weren't dependent on such support, additional untapped sources of income, and certain other helpful circumstances.

The institutions in financial difficulty reacted to the cost-income squeeze by postponing expansions and new program growth and by implementing general belt-tightening measures (cutting and freezing expenditures), cutting and reallocating resources between departments and programs, searching for new revenues, and planning and worrying about next steps.

*Two organizations important for attempting to codify the procedures and concepts of institutional cost studies are the National Center for Higher Education Management Systems (in Boulder, Colo.) and the National Association of College and University Business Officers (in Washington, D.C.). Both hold many relevant publications with periodic updates and conduct training workshops.

Many private institutions used deficit financing. Five significant cost stimuli were reported: inflation, faculty salaries, student aid, campus disturbances, and growth in responsibilities, activities, and aspirations. These problems sound familiar 20 years later.

In 1973, Cheit revisited the 41 schools in the original study and found a fragile stability. Clark Kerr in the foreword to the follow-up report stated:

> *The reduction of the rate of increase of costs has been almost phenomenal. In terms of rising expenditure per student per year above the general rate of inflation, the rate of increase for this group of institutions has gone down from nearly 4.0 percent in the earlier period to 0.5 percent* (p. v).

It is important to note that the second report provides a record of real adaptation by institutions to controlling and reducing costs. Also, it is in this report that Cheit describes the kind of adaptation that was occurring: "The method of change is by substitution or even contraction, but not by growth" (p. 73). Kerr calls this the hardest kind of change strategy. Change by substitution (in other words, internal reallocation of resources) is advocated today as the principal means of adaptation (Zemsky and Massy 1990).

Rounding out this brief review of some of the important literature about the management of costs are two books with similar emphases. The older, *The Managerial Revolution in Higher Education* (Rourke and Brooks 1966), found higher education institutions adopting new management methods to increase both their efficiency and effectiveness. What they found was this:

> *In place of the loose, unstructured, and somewhat casual methods of management practiced . . . in the past, we have seen a growing commitment to the use of automation in the routine processes of administration, an increased resort to data gathering and research as a basis for policy making, and an expanding effort to develop objective criteria for making decisions on the allocation of resources instead of leaving these matters entirely to the play of campus pressures or the force of tradition* (p. vi).

The results of the study, gathered from questionnaires sent to more than 400 state institutions and interviews with more than 200 individuals at 33 colleges and universities, led Rourke and Brooks to conclude that a managerial revolution was taking place. Computerization and institutional research were seen to play key roles in these changes.

Another view on this subject was titled *Academic Strategy: The Management Revolution in American Higher Education* (Keller 1983). Keller wrote about the planning and management revolution overtaking higher education 17 years after Rourke and Brooks. He especially was concerned with the application of strategic planning to the mounting problems of higher education: "A specter is haunting higher education: the specter of decline and bankruptcy" (p. 3) was his opening line. Keller saw a need for leaders, administrators, staff, and faculty to perceive and act on the necessity to reformulate the administration of higher education. In 1990, he told a doctoral student in the Higher Education Program at Florida State University that he most regretted that many institutions had failed to connect planning with budgeting, the link necessary to make strategic planning work. And so the need for better management continues, especially during a recession.

"A specter is haunting higher education: the specter of decline and bankruptcy."

Organization of This Report
This monograph is not primarily concerned with the issue of rising tuitions, although it does identify one of the important components of tuition growth: costs and expenditures. How costs are managed—ways the actions and decisions are made to control, reduce, increase, and account for institutional expenditures and costs—is the primary focus.

The next three sections of this monograph cover the main topics related to managing costs in higher education. The section titled "The Influence of Revenues on Costs" examines some of the more prominent issues about the circumstances in which costs are generated by revenues and how the major sources of revenues have changed and affected costs.

The section following "Revenues" focuses on "Costs and Cost Pressures." It is a review of the external and internal cost factors, the dynamics of change, and the nature of institutional responses. What are these pressures, and can they be managed? For prognostications about future costs, one should consult the 1990 publications cited above and note that none anticipated a recession of any depth or duration.

The third section focuses on "Managing and Controlling Costs." Major revenue and cost problems are described, typical reactions noted, and the secondary consequences identified and examined. Mini-case materials are used to illustrate the various reactions. The management strategies, tactics, and practices used to control costs in both "ordinary" times and financial emergencies are presented.

The last section, "Cost Management Practices," summarizes the cost management approaches reported and recommends a set of procedures for better cost control. Although the tone here is more prescriptive, these are general approaches to this important management and administrative activity. We have yet to find a single cost management recipe or silver bullet that will serve all the needs of higher education. But many approaches are available to those who want to systematically control costs.

THE INFLUENCE OF REVENUES ON COSTS

In this section the nature of the relationship between revenues and costs first is examined. Then, each major source of revenues is identified and its impact on costs assessed. Although greater revenues might be needed for worthy educational purposes, it is not assumed that increased revenues will lead to a better management of costs. Following is a brief description of the revenue-cost nexus.

The relationship of revenues to costs oftentimes is direct, sometimes obscure. The purpose for which revenues are received usually establishes the unit level of costs for a program. The ability to manage these costs often is constrained by restrictions placed on revenues. The demands to implement programs not fully funded might artificially hold down costs and prevent quality program development.

At other times, new programs might receive revenues by taking them from older programs, a process of internal reallocation. The Carnegie Commission on Higher Education claimed the latter was an appropriate strategy for the 1970s; it might be widely practiced in the 1990s (1972). Internal reallocation, now called growth by substitution, results in an internal shifting of costs as well as revenues (Zemsky and Massy 1990; Cheit 1973).

The Revenue Theory of Costs

In 1980, Howard Bowen defined a fundamental relationship between revenues and costs: "The basic concept underlying the revenue theory of cost is that an institution's educational costs per student unit is determined by the revenues available for educational purposes" (p. 17). Thus, the greater the revenues, the greater the cost or funds expended. Bowen deduced five "laws" from his theory:

1. The dominant goals of institutions are educational excellence, prestige, and influence.
2. In quest of excellence, prestige, and influence, there is virtually no limit to the amount of money an institution could spend for seemingly fruitful educational needs.
3. Each institution raises all the money it can.
4. Each institution spends all it raises.
5. The cumulative effect of the preceding four laws is toward ever-increasing expenditure (pp. 19-20).

Although Bowen was concerned with instructional unit costs, his codification of the relationships between revenues and costs has explanatory power across most activities in colleges and universities. It is practically an iron law that nonprofit organizations will attempt each year to spend every dollar they receive. In much of the nonprofit sector, arrival at the end of the fiscal year with funds unspent and uncommitted (unencumbered) often is looked on as evidence of poor managerial ability (or padded budget requests) rather than good financial stewardship. In nonprofit organizations, no rewards are offered for "saving" revenues as would be offered in the profit sector.

Another reason for the absence of funds at the end of the fiscal year is that nonprofit organizations always have a long list of unmet needs and underfunded programs. The list of unmet needs in higher education grows during the years when government spending is reduced (relatively or absolutely); the list lengthens when technologies change, new demands emerge (to facilitate state economic development, for example), and old resources have to be augmented or replaced just to sustain current operations. The postponement or deferral of the maintenance of equipment and facilities, which inevitably results in greater costs in the future, illustrates the dilemma facing many underfunded colleges and universities.

Funding Higher Education's Goals
When resources are available, governments, corporations, and individuals provide financial support to colleges and universities so valued social goals might be achieved. The goals include socialization into a broader culture, education to perpetuate the political and economic system, training for employment, generating new knowledge and technology, and many other purposes. The elixir of higher education is thought to perpetuate the social classes *and* facilitate social mobility, broaden and deepen the understanding of the young, and provide the high technology that will make American goods more competitive in the world market.

One of the unique social purposes expected of colleges and universities is the identification and nurturing of talent. The various programs to recruit students and then provide them financial assistance, guidance and counseling, learning resources, good instruction, and job placement opportunities indicate how extensive this commitment has become. American institutions providing a vast array of services generate a need for revenues from a great variety of sources, since no single benefactor pays the cost of an entire service or all services provided by an institution.

External sources of funds are governments, foundations, business and industry, individual donors, alumni, parents, and the clients of college and university programs. Clients demand services and offer resources in exchange. In the process, if the demanded services cost more than the resources offered, then some way must be found to bring them into balance. In response, the services demanded can be restricted, the offered resources increased, existing resources reallocated from ongoing programs, or revenues increased from other sources. These broadly negotiated arrangements (many through governing boards or legislatures) should be contrasted with the limited options available when programs are mandated.

In some instances, external sources mandate programs or services and fail to adequately, fully, or even partially fund their mandates. State and federal government demands based on old social policy (such as social security) and new social policy oftentime fall in this category—accountability reporting, building access for the disabled, implementing new health and safety standards, energy conservation, and recycling, for example.

Another demand, like a mandate (from a variety of sources but especially governments), is to offer contracts for services but not pay full overhead costs, or to restrict the amount of overhead to exclude such elements as publishing reports. In these instances, the offer of resources for some service is made on a "take it or leave it" basis. Government actions in these matters might result from shrinking revenues from taxpayers or a change in attitude about higher education.

The current pattern of reduced government funding is, according to Robert M. Rosenzweig, president of the American Association of Universities, more than a temporary problem:

> *There has been a sea change in the views of policy makers in the United States and Western Europe about the financing of higher education. It takes different forms in different places, but the overriding fact is that governments now expect more from their universities but want to pay less for it* (1990, p. A44).

In the same vein but at the state level, legislators in Florida in 1990-91 began to question whether they wanted to fund the expanded missions of community colleges beyond the historic purpose of preparing students to transfer to four-year institutions and postsecondary education for individuals with special needs. The belief that higher education is involved in too many activities and doesn't place enough emphasis on instructing undergraduates well is voiced by many individuals and legislators. Many state governments place a higher priority on undergraduate instruction in universities than on graduate education and research. Falling state revenues might stimulate a review of institutional missions and priorities in relation to those of government.

Changes in the economy cause ripples throughout higher education (Anderson and Meyerson 1990). Reductions in discretionary income to individuals and the rising cost of higher education influence the choice of institution. A slowing economy, due to such factors as rising oil prices, moderate inflation, stubborn interest rates, and other economic problems reduces the value of tax revenues paid to all levels of government. Higher education frequently feels the double pinch of declining state revenues and lower purchasing power because of inflation. Similarly, falling government aid to students, whether relative or absolute, further compounds the situation.

It is not only the strength of the economy as the basis for taxes that is important to higher education. The economy is the destination of most of the graduates of colleges and universities. However, a belief persists that the United States has an excess number of college graduates and that these graduates are taking jobs that formerly would have been filled by high school graduates. A recent report estimated that "the pool of college graduates exceeds by about 15 percent the need for their skills in professions that require college training, among them engineering, accounting, law, and medicine" (Uchitelle 1990; see also the hypercritical report by Freeman 1976).

However, the "overeducated" college graduates were being hired because their degrees indicated to employers that these people had such qualities as punctuality, good work habits, and the ability to learn on the job. No other industrial society has so many college graduates. Many observers believe this situation is a waste of consumer and taxpayer funds. The image projected is that parts of higher education can be both personally expensive and socially wasteful, even though it is providing a useful and needed service.

Demographic Change and Costs

A reduction in the number of undergraduate students tends to drive up instructional costs. This especially is true at colleges and universities in which the faculties are heavily tenured, the emphasis has been on undergraduate instruction, and small classes have been the norm. At research universities, such a decrease likely will reduce the support available for graduate students, since fewer teaching and lab assistants will be needed.

In addition, the extra revenue from undergraduate tuition and state instructional subsidies would decline and reduce the support for both funded and unfunded research, a challenge to the mission of a research institution. The costs of instruction could increase if research faculty are called to teach more, for researchers tend to be paid higher salaries and come from higher cost disciplines. Low enrollments and small class sizes lead to rising costs.

Another consequence of actual or anticipated decline in the number of undergraduate students is that institutions add to their administrative costs. Such costs automatically would rise if the share of administrative costs is allocated across a decreasing number of students. For example, institutions might expand their student-recruitment activities into a full-fledged marketing program, which includes adding staff, hiring consultants, improving and increasing advertising, visiting more high schools, cultivating alumni and friends of the institution in a more sophisticated manner, and so on. Private colleges have been developing and perfecting their marketing programs for many years as they attempt to cope effectively with the demographic swings of the 1990s.

Another response to declining enrollments is to expand services and facilities to make the institutions more attractive. The private colleges that appeal to a financially well-off clientele might add everything from riding stables to international tours as part of the educational experience. However, large public institutions might offer large student unions, beautiful grounds, and leisure-sports complexes rivaling commercial sports centers. In this vein also are the expanded intercollegiate-sports facilities at many private and public institutions that support national football, basketball, or other sports—many for both men and women.

The expenditures on sports are believed to bring increased visibility and, indirectly, more revenues. Of course, the costs of top football teams can rise so high that even though a university generates millions in sports revenues, this might not be enough to keep the athletic department out of debt. The ambition to be the best indeed is costly. On the other hand, a very successful sports program can make substantial funding contributions to academic programs and general student scholarships.

Revenue from Tuition and Student Aid

The principal revenue sources examined below include tuition and student financial aid. Federal and state support and gifts and endowments are described in subsequent sections.

Tuition and student aid

Tuition is the price charged the student for instruction and educational programs. It is not the total cost of education, for few institutions could charge full cost and enroll the number of students needed to make the institution economically viable. Low tuition at public two- and four-year institutions is designed to make a higher education available to all who are qualified.

Tuition ranges from 20-35 percent of the cost of instruction at public institutions to 55-70 percent at private schools. A variety of sources subsidize the cost of instruction, including benefactors, state and local governments, student financial aid providers, and the institutions themselves through investments. Clearly, an important link exists between tuition and student aid.

Although tuition is the price of instruction to students, it is not always a single fixed amount (even when differentiated by level of education). Colleges offer discounts or reductions to their basic tuition rates; both public and private colleges and two-year institutions offer them. The discounts are provided to recruit students, to implement some mandated public benefit, and to keep a desired mix of programs and faculty. When a college makes exceptions to its stated tuition rates, two effects can occur: Its potential revenues and funds for other programs are reduced, and costs are shifted from partial-paying students to those who can pay the posted price. These reductions are targeted to various groups, for example: the children of alumni, multiple members of the same family, the children of professors in private colleges, children of deceased fire fighters, police officers, or veterans, people over age 65, convicts, and others. In graduate institutions, tuition remission might be offered to graduate students who provide services such as teaching or research assistance to an institution. At public institutions, such discounts might include a waiver of out-of-state fees for nonresidents as well.

These price discounts are not to be confused with the scholarships, fellowships, and assistantships provided to undergraduate and graduate students; often these awards also make the recipient eligible to receive a tuition discount. Student aid and fee waivers (discounts) are offered in combination to undergraduate students with special talents in such areas as academics, athletics, music (the marching band, for example), performing arts, and special occupational categories. These total-aid packages specifically might be used to bring a variety of talents and backgrounds to a campus. A problematic aspect of some financial aid awards is generated if the funds are used for no-need scholarships or fee reductions. Conversely, the funds are judged to be used more appropriately when awarded to students who have a genuine financial need, especially if such individuals are highly talented and/or minority students. However, it should be clear as reported previously that multiple uses exist for student aid.

Labeling the lost revenue from the price reductions as a cost is crucial when an institution decides to devote an increasing share of its unrestricted current funds to financial aid. Price discounts can be treated as revenue reductions rather than costs when the institution makes no attempt to transfer funds from a nontuition source to the tuition revenue fund for the discounts. However, spending funds for student aid that have been obtained from the unrestricted general fund constitutes a cost, especially if the funds could have been used for other purposes (see Hauptman 1990). Herein lies a significant issue aside from the accounting procedures. The additional expenditure for student aid may come partially or wholly from the revenues generated from increased tuition— those who can pay the regular tuition will be partially subsidizing those who cannot pay full price. This internal redistribution of tuition income may be seen as an unfair "tax" on full-paying parents, many of whom also would object to paying increased income taxes just for higher education.

Tuition investments. A recent innovation open to people who want to save money for the future higher education of children is the fixed-tuition contract. Such contracts result when a prospective student's family or benefactor makes a lump-sum deposit (or time payments) some years in advance to purchase one to four years of future tuition at *current* prices.

Institutions (and states) that have such plans are speculating that the interest earned on the advance payments will be enough to cover the tuition charged in the future. A decline in the market for investments, rising inflation, and reduced funding by governments (which could necessitate a significant increase in tuition) make this plan risky for institutions. Both private and public institutions that use these plans could have to pay large costs in the future because the prepaid funds and income will be insufficient to cover future costs.

The fact is that very few financial managers or institutional administrators accurately can forecast interest rates or higher education costs fifteen, ten, five, or even three years in advance. A further complication that results from this plan is that its existence might place political restrictions on the management of institutional revenues and budgets. For example, when public university presidents in Florida called for a tuition increase, objections immediately arose from the manager of the state's prepaid tuition fund. This shows that a well-intended idea can result in undesirable secondary consequences for institutions. Successful programs of this kind which do not restrict an institution's ability to raise tuition are to be commended, but then who will pay a future deficit between the tuition contract and the new tuition price?

Tuition charges and increases

Table 1 is created from data published in the 1988 *Digest of Education Statistics* and illustrates the charges to students in 1987-88. It also indicates the magnitude of differences between degree programs and institutional control. Charges for the current year would be larger.

Between 1973-74 and 1985-86, the price of higher education to students at public institutions rose by 143 percent at a university, 149 percent at four-year colleges, and 135 percent for

1987-88 CHARGES TO STUDENTS

	Tuition and Fees			Tuition and Fees Plus All Charges		
	2-year	4-year	University	2-year	4-year	University
Private	$3,910	6,670	8,770	6,870	10,050	13,330
Public	$690	1,320	1,750	3,230	4,130	4,760

two-year colleges. In the private institutions, the increases were 199 percent for universities, 179 percent for four-year colleges, and 166 percent for two-year colleges (Hartle 1986).

During the 1970s, the increase in tuition was below the rate of inflation, but during the 1980s it was above the rate measured by the Consumer Price Index. The rate of increase in tuition at private institutions regularly exceeds the increase for public colleges and universities. Frances in 1990 reported that the rate of tuition increase has declined substantially since 1981-82, when the rise for private institutions was 12.5 percent; this then fell to 8 percent in 1987-88. The decrease was larger for the public-sector institutions: It fell from almost 9 percent to 5 percent during the same period.

College administrators who want to increase tuition revenue may undertake a number of curricular and structural changes including everything from making two-year institutions into four-year colleges to adding a business management minor for liberal arts students. When administrators overfocus their attention on the revenue potential of their solution, they fail to consider the costs. That is, adding students might require adding part-time or full-time faculty, library materials, financial aid, and a variety of services. Such future costs must be anticipated and managed if the expected increase in revenue is to help cover preexisting costs.

When administrators overfocus their attention on the revenue potential of their solution, they fail to consider the costs.

Student financial aid

Since 1970, according to estimates, more than $200 billion has been spent on student financial aid; by the early 1980s, the amount spent each year had reached nearly $20 billion (Wittstruck 1988). Annual financial aid now is estimated at nearly $30 billion (Hauptman 1991). A portion of this aid is used to pay tuition, which in turn helps pay part of the cost of instruction.

Student financial aid, while increasing 218 percent during the 1970s, increased by only 21 percent during the 1980s. This translates to a decrease of 6 percent after adjusting for inflation (Hansen 1988). The relative decline in the growth of aid stimulated many private institutions to increase the share of revenues they spent on student financial aid. "Institutions had more than doubled the amount of aid they provided from their own resources between 1979-80 and 1986-87" (Hauptman 1990, p. 73); the increase rose from $2.2 billion to $5.2 billion. Such aid might constitute 20 to 25 percent of student financial aid. These data indicate that the external sources of aid—such as the federal government, which funds 73 percent of aid—have not kept pace with the growing demand for aid. In fact, declining federal aid might have stimulated tuition increases. That kind of result is the opposite of the relationship touted by former Secretary of Education William Bennett.

The tuition-student aid nexus. Various assertions have been made about the relationship between costs, student financial aid, and tuition charges. One version, propounded by Bennett, asserts that as the federal government increased financial aid, institutions raised their fees to capture the increased aid monies. The implication is that a rise in federal aid stimulated a rise in costs. President William Bowen of Princeton wrote in 1987 that he believed mostly the for-profit sector of postsecondary education might show such a tendency (*Higher Education Costs* 1988). Subsequent reports in Congress and elsewhere confirmed Bowen's thesis.

Early estimates for 1989-90 are that the federal government supplied about 73 percent of student financial aid ("Flash-card" 1990); this number is down from 78 percent estimated for 1984-85 (Andrew and Russo 1989) and 83 percent in 1980-81. In 1984-85, the federal government was in the last stages of phasing out direct student aid to social security dependents and veterans. State student aid was estimated to be 6 percent in 1989-90, 7 percent in 1984-85, and 5 percent in 1980-81. The remainder, institutional aid, was estimated at 21 percent in 1989-90, 15 percent in 1984-85, and 12 percent in 1980-81. No local aid was reported. As can be seen, the fastest growing aid component was from colleges and universities; other estimates maintained that institutions might be providing 25 percent of the student financial aid (Frances 1990).

Federal Support of Higher Education
The federal government is not only the largest single supplier of student financial aid but also the largest source of funds

for research. An official estimate for fiscal year 1990 shows $9.6 billion for student aid, $3.3 billion for other postsecondary programs, $13 billion for research, and about $2 billion for other special programs. In addition, the student aid programs generate $11.3 billion of support from state agencies, institutions, and private sources (*Federal Support for Education* 1991, pp. 14-15). Very few federal dollars are awarded directly to fund the cost of instruction, although some funds may be targeted for certain critical fields. Even though monies from federal sources are significant and necessary, they are not consistent sources of revenue. Their reduction has a profound effect on student educational opportunity and the production of basic research and development in the nation. Following are major expenditures of federal funds.

Student assistance

Student financial aid is an important means by which to recruit college youth who are talented but who lack sufficient resources. It also is a means by which to recruit minorities and others who can provide the multicultural environment for a campus that mirrors the larger society. Presently, one-third of all need-based financial aid recipients are considered minority-group members (Stampen and Fenske 1988).

The nature of federal student aid has changed dramatically in the past 15 years. In 1975-76, grants accounted for 80 percent of all student aid; their share declined to 56 percent in 1980-81 and then to 49 percent in 1988-89 (Hartle 1990). Grants are very important in enrolling disadvantaged and minority students. Unfortunately, grants might not be achieving their public policy objectives:

> *Persistence is a serious problem in both public and independent higher education, particularly for black and Hispanic students. The dirty secret of the Pell [Grant] Program is that half of all recipients never complete any academic program* (Saunders 1991, p. B2).*

---

* These and other facts about the federal programs will be considered in 1992 when Congress renews the Higher Education Act. Saunders believes major changes might be in the wings; proposals are to be made by Lamar Alexander, the secretary of education. The emphasis might shift to providing funds to those institutions with the best management records in the use of student aid monies.

Federal student aid programs for the disadvantaged were established through the Higher Education Act of 1965. Need-based grant programs for the disadvantaged began then along with government-guaranteed private bank loans for middle-class students (Gladieux 1989). The Equal Opportunity Grant Program of the federal government passed in 1972. These programs increased minority enrollment substantially (Astin 1982); minority participation continued to rise until the late 1970s. The shift in the 1980s from grants to loans, as described earlier, has required low-income and minority students to select loans as their means of college finance.

Unfortunately, the shift has led to decreased minority enrollments, increasing defaults on loans by students from low-income families, and other undesirable consequences. However, some evidence proves the programs work. For example, Wilson (1990) reports a study that revealed that almost 93 percent of black students who received grants still were enrolled after the first year, compared with only 66 percent who did not receive grants. Whereas the right types of aid can help students persist in college, these positive relationships might decline over the years of attendance—and many of these students will not receive a degree (Jensen 1981, 1984; Leslie and Brinkman 1988).

Another important policy issue about federal student aid centers on the default rates of federally guaranteed loans. The rates have caused any number of problems for both majority and minority students and the institutions involved. Federal government officials and members of Congress also have been widely criticized for allowing the rates to rise and stay so high. According to *Business Officer* (1991, p. 7), the average default rate is about 17 percent; proprietary trade schools average 27 percent. Defaulted loans have grown from $151 million in 1981 to $2.7 billion in 1991. The federal government now is removing the eligibility of students for these loans if an institution's default rate exceeds 30 percent.

Research projects, equipment, and facilities

Six major agencies of the federal government support research in universities: the National Science Foundation, the National Institutes of Health, the National Aeronautics and Space Administration, and the departments of agriculture, defense, education, and energy. The Department of Health and Human Services funds the most research (*Federal Support for Edu-*

cation 1991, p. 8). A variety of committees in both the U.S. House and Senate oversee the research programs and their appropriations; several national associations of universities monitor and lobby for research funding.

The primary purpose behind federal support of university research is to underwrite the long-term development of fundamental knowledge. The government realizes that about two-thirds of the basic research in the United States occurs on university campuses. This fact alone leads the national military establishment to support university research as a potential contribution to national security. Technological development, world economic competition, health, safety, and many other factors stimulate federal support of research.

Another and equally important objective is to support the training of the next generation of scientists. However, the research resources provided by the federal government to colleges and universities have changed significantly. For example, "Federal funding of academic research—including the associated equipment—grew at an average annual rate of 15.7 percent, in constant dollars, during 1953-1967, but the rate fell to 1.6 percent during 1968-1983" (*University Research Infrastructure* 1986, p. 463). From 1983 to 1990, university research (constant) funds increased from $9 billion to $13 billion or about 5 percent annually (*Federal Support for Education* 1991, p. 8). In 1983, federal funding of $4.96 billion (current dollars) constituted about 64 percent of academic research and development; state and local government funded about 7 percent, industry 5 percent, universities 16 percent, and other sources 8 percent (*University Research Infrastructure* 1986, p. 475).

The needs of many other federal programs have prevented an expansion of federal support for civilian research at universities. Since 1980, nondefense research and development funds increased by 59 percent, but defense-related research expanded by 191 percent (Hartle 1990). The United States is losing out to France, Germany, Japan, and the United Kingdom, countries that devote a far larger share of their governmental budgets on research to advance fundamental knowledge (p. 36). It should not be surprising to U.S. officials that American universities are looking for research funds from these other countries. In the early 1990s, the possibility of gaining a "peace dividend" by reducing defense spending was being examined for its net effect on research funding—

it could result in a decrease in defense-related research but perhaps lead to modest increases in basic research funding. Unfortunately, the Gulf War stifled the peace dividend. Now that the war is over, the unfortunate consequences of the recession are rapidly absorbing the cuts in defense spending.

Project funding. Project funding of research, the primary method, raises several issues. First among them is that the federal government and many other sources fail to fund the full costs of research. America's research universities are highly dependent upon the federal government for research funding, and they use the funds to enhance the research enterprise as well as to conduct particular research projects. Here is how a national university study group explained to Congress the funding benefits and the shortcomings of the federal grants system:

> *Federal funds help to house and conduct the project in an already existing institutional environment. Federal funds leverage institutional resources and may trigger other third-party support. Unlike industry, universities do not receive independent research and development funds (IR&D). Universities build their own capacity through independent research and instruction from which their research base is developed. . . . It allows [institutional leaders] to bring to bear the concentration of a small group on a particular project for a brief period of time (University Research Infrastructure 1986, pp. 297-8).*

What is at issue is that when a university already has a staff, facilities, equipment, and a commitment to undertake research, administrators believe they should be recompensed; if the institution didn't have these resources, it would have to seek additional funds to build an appropriate research capacity. Universities find that the costs of all of these existing resources need to be charged to projects funded from external sources; however, administrators are not always permitted to do so by the various federal rules and the conflicting interpretations of them. Unfortunately, the Congressional Budget Office believes that the unclear regulations, poor executive agency supervision, and the rising need of the research universities for funds have led to abuses of the system of federal grants and contracts (see *Chronicle of Higher Education* February 5, 1992, p. 1).

Equipment. The federal government has provided during the past two decades a majority share of the funds used by the universities for the purchase of research equipment. A National Science Foundation survey of equipment in use in 1982-83 revealed that the equipment was funded 54 percent by the federal government, 32 percent by universities, 5 percent by state governments, and 9 percent from private and other sources (Chaudhari 1986). In 1985, the National Science Foundation allocated about 20 percent of its funds for research equipment, most of which was part of larger project grants. Unfortunately, "the government's annual spending on academic R&D facilities and equipment, in constant dollars, fell some 78 percent during 1966-1983" (*University Research Infrastructure* 1986, p. 463).

By 1985 and through 1988, various federal agencies including the Department of Defense began to increase the size of grants allowed for scientific instruments. By the late 1980s, funding again obviously was insufficient; special funding for equipment was being proposed in the U.S. House in the spring of 1990. The climbing federal deficit—the interest on which would amount to more than the entire defense budget for 1990-91—gave little hope for more than modest funding in this area. However, Congress has been expanding its overall research appropriations in the 1990s.

In addition to the direct role of the federal government in funding scientific equipment, Congress has passed laws which encourage gifts of equipment to colleges and universities. For example, the Economic Recovery Tax Act of 1981 encouraged manufacturers, through tax deductions, to make charitable gifts of scientific equipment to universities. In 1983-1984, about $117 million of company products were donated to colleges and universities. However, the tax reform act of 1986 reduced this incentive by changing the impact of these deductions on the net taxes to be paid by donors.

Although the problems of limited resources have been recognized, some White House science advisors stated in 1985 that the universities had become too dependent on federal resources for research support and that the universities needed to abandon their passive stance and seek other funding for research. Since that time, a number of research universities have conducted capital-fund drives in which sizable portions are earmarked for research equipment and facilities. Expanded research contracted with industry is another source for new equipment funding.

Facilities. There is a need to rebuild academic research facilities, a move which is expected to cost about $10 billion. The federal government has supported facilities construction and improvement over the years, but that too has changed. In 1967, about $700 million was supplied colleges and universities; in 1990, it was about $70 million (Hartle 1990, p. 37). In 1991, NSF alone awarded $39 million to 78 colleges and universities in 37 states to fund repair and renovation of laboratories and other research facilities. The need for federal revenue remains crucial for all of the purposes it supports.

State Subsidies and Student Assistance

State subsidies to public institutions are provided to keep tuition low enough so that all who are qualified may benefit from a college education, whether two-year, four-year, or graduate. State financial aid to students serves the same purpose—to facilitate access—but also is extended to students who attend private, more costly, institutions. For 1988, it was estimated that the states spent nearly $63 billion on higher education.

One of the newer funding arrangements between state government and private higher education involves contracting for programs. States may fund specific programs at private colleges or universities instead of duplicating programs on nearby public campuses. Medical programs and others may be included. State consortia such as the Western Interstate Commission for Higher Education also collaborate to avoid creating highly specialized programs—such as psychiatric nursing—in every state. The host state extends in-state tuition schedules to any student from the region who enrolls in these programs.

One of the major changes in the state funding of higher education has been the use of various methods to target funds for particular purposes such as quality improvement. A 1989 study summarized in five categories the principal methods used:

1. Incentive or performance funding tied to such goals as educational improvement, assessment, fund-raising, and

business partnerships.
2. Categorical funding for targeted academic programs or for institutional or statewide centers of excellence.
3. Competitive grants for research projects and quality improvement.
4. Financial deregulation and other funding flexibility mechanisms tied to quality improvement.
5. Formula funding adjustments for quality enhancements such as no loss of revenues due to decreased enrollments (Berdahl and Studds 1989, p. 2).

As these special funding categories grow, institutions will have to become skilled at preparing proposals to maximize the revenues available, for incentive grants might constitute the principal means by which to obtain new monies. Note that the states might perform evaluation studies to see if the funds were used properly and if the desired results were obtained. As one state legislator put it, "These are not more 'take the money and run' deals for institutions; they will have to be accountable for the funds and the promised results" (Berdahl and Studds 1989, p. 17).

In addition to state subsidies and student assistance, the states have many funding controls over public higher education. They can approve programs, budget requests, tuition levels, construction funding, and many other details. Governors and state legislatures can act jointly to close public colleges, a policy rarely proposed except when state revenues are declining precipitously. The persistent recession of 1990-1992 has revived this possibility (see Massachusetts, for example).

State legislators from the hometowns of the threatened institutions usually manage to stave off the death of their local public college. However, the American Association of State Colleges and Universities is reported to have found in its annual budget survey that "things will get worse (perhaps much worse) before they get better" ("State Notes" 1991, p. 5). By April 1991, 18 states had cut current higher education appropriations, while five states offered some increases (Samuelson 1991). At least 27 states had to make changes after the legislative appropriations process was completed. In many states, tuition and fees were increased to raise additional money.

States reacted by using nonrecurring revenues and contingency funds to cover the shortfall in revenues during 1990-91. Then they proposed to cut continuing programs and staff throughout state government for the 1991-92 and 1992-93 years. Because education, including higher education, consumes the largest share of expenditures by state government, the funding for colleges and universities has and will be trimmed. Even state student financial aid is expected to be reduced in some states. More than $2.151 billion of such aid was to be awarded by states in 1990-91. Colleges will be sorely tested to find alternate sources of student aid funds to keep up with the almost certain tuition increases.

Another state responsibility related to finances involves review and/or approval of grant applications to the federal government. Over the last two decades, the federal government's Education Department has required postsecondary grant applications from colleges and universities in each state to be processed through a state agency—usually the state department of education. The purpose is to allow states to plan how federal funds ought to be distributed within. The consequences of this process are yet to be investigated: For example, does it enhance or restrict institutional funding opportunities? The federal student aid programs of Perkins Loans, Pell Grants, and College Work-Study were exempt from this requirement in 1990.

State general funds for higher education
The adequacy of state financing for higher education is a regular concern with the many constituencies of public and private colleges and universities. During times of reduced state economic activity, government officials face the challenge of slowing the increase in appropriations or needing to cut back current allocations to colleges and universities. In the normal legislative session, a reduction or a stand-still appropriation creates substantial political feedback from parents and students and generates pressure to increase funds for higher education. In these negotiations, institutions are asked to become more efficient, cut out frills and duplicate programs, and increase productivity—perhaps by requiring faculty to teach more undergraduate courses and larger classes, for example.

Cost consciousness and conservation are urged upon the institutions. Reducing costs and expenditures is advocated by various state officials and a variety of business-related interest groups such as chambers of commerce, tax-watch groups, and those who believe that the beneficiaries of higher education should pay a larger share of the total cost of higher education.

What hurts public higher education the most in periods of economic deterioration is when state government fails to correctly forecast economic conditions and appropriates funds on the basis of an optimistic rate of tax collections. Public institutions tend to follow the lead of the state government and make financial plans that also can be too optimistic; pressure to make this mistake is especially great in states with increasing populations and enrollments or even those with decreasing enrollments. Then when revenues fail to grow as projected or show no increase at all, the states must freeze expenditures and even cut appropriations. If institutions haven't set aside reserves for these contingencies, then institutional budgets must be frozen and cut as quickly as possible—which usually means the following semester.

Institutional reactions to these financial emergencies are typically short-term; rarely are changes made in the management of financial resources. This experience should make it clear that an institution's desire for state support should be tempered by an understanding that the economic forecasts of states might be only modestly reliable.

In a large number of states, what happens financially to the public institutions through state action has a secondary effect on the private institutions. For example, private institutions in a state might set their salary levels in relation to salaries in the public institutions. This might be a reasonable response to labor-market conditions so that faculty are not paid so poorly in the small private colleges that they migrate to a higher paying public institution. Private institutions that use this strategy need to be aware of the difficulties states face in accurately forecasting the economic future and appropriations. A further complication for private higher education exists in states which provide student credit-hour subsidies; state allocations might be cut substantially the next fiscal year after a year-old revenue shortfall.

The response of public institutions to mid-year appropriation cutbacks, rarely disclosed in detail, can be significantly creative when anticipated. For example, if these institutions find that they must forfeit faculty and staff positions (along with their salaries), it would be wise to assess the likelihood

What hurts public higher education the most in periods of economic deterioration is when state government fails to correctly forecast economic conditions. . . .

of position replacements. If it is slightly easier to receive funding for faculty rather than staff positions, then perhaps "returning" more faculty positions would be wise. These and many other insightful arrangements might be attempted to offset some of the pain of state financial retrenchment.

State funding of research

States depend upon the federal government to fund basic research. However, states do fund special projects with a very specific focus (economic development institutes or solar energy research centers, for example) and frequently are willing to appropriate matching and development funds to compete for large federally sponsored research centers, such as Star Wars projects, a nuclear accelerator, or supercomputers. States frequently finance new research equipment when they build or renovate laboratories; some are providing matching funds for federal equipment and facilities awards. Many states have unrealistic expectations about the life of research and other equipment which they want to last as long as the building in which it is housed. Such restrictions reduce the possibility of state institutions continuing to conduct research at the frontiers of knowledge.

A host of state regulations reduce the flexibility of most state institutions to adequately fund, manage, or plan long-range research programs. Private universities have much greater flexibility in all areas and are able to respond rapidly to emerging research opportunities. A study reported in a 1986 congressional document indicated that even public universities with a greater degree of autonomy tended to depend less on state support for research and more on federal and private sources (*University Research Infrastructure*, p. 523). A widespread feeling exists among state university research administrators that compliance with state purchasing requirements costs more than if each university or a consortium of institutions were to carry out its own procurement activities for the highly specialized equipment and supplies required for research and teaching scientific subjects.

It should be noted that when institutions report their share of the cost of research projects and equipment, portions of that cost may be underwritten with state funds appropriated generally for education. A few state legislators are suspicious that funds intended for undergraduate instruction are being used in public institutions for graduate teaching and research to the neglect of the undergraduates. Questions by legislative staff about the number of centers and institutes in a public university might indicate the concern that not enough is being spent on undergraduate instruction.

Gifts, Grants, and Endowment Income

Private or independent collegiate institutions depend more on gifts, grants, and endowment income than do public colleges and universities. However, as state resources stabilize or actually decline in relation to inflation as well as functional need, public institutions increasingly have sought funds from philanthropic sources.

One of the complex issues with cost implications for these kinds of revenues is the demand for divestiture of certain stocks and bonds. Over the years, peace and justice groups have demanded that colleges and universities divest themselves of stocks from companies that make armaments or conduct business with South Africa. More recently, suggestions or demands have been made by health officials (in California, for example), citizen health groups, and anti-smoking groups that higher education divest itself of tobacco stocks. Proponents argue that health and moral issues are involved. Rice University President George Rupp is reported to oppose such action because tobacco stock has been a strong performer and would be one of the best consumer-products investments in the 1990s (*Chronicle of Higher Education*, 1991, p. A27). Shutting off needed revenue is a difficult choice; disposing of stocks when the market is unpredictable or sliding down could cause an important loss of gift, grant, and endowment funds. Each institution must decide whether these substantive demands are worth a potentially uneconomical action.

Gifts and grants

Gifts by individuals and corporations to higher education fluctuate according to the state of the economy, changes in the tax laws, and the relatedness of the gifts to the needs of various institutions. Gifts declined in 1987-88 because of the substantial drop in the stock market during October 1987 and the full implementation of the 1986 changes in the federal tax laws. The very large market decline scared investors badly. The new tax laws removed several deductions for charitable giving and reduced the impact of the remaining deductions because of the lower tax rates. As a result, private giving declined for the first time in 10 years.

However, for 1988-89, the Council for Aid to Education (CFAE) reported that gifts had increased 8.8 percent to a record $8.9 billion. According to CFAE, all categories of private giving showed increases: Alumni donations rose 12.2 percent; nonalumni giving, 7.8 percent; corporate donations, 5.1 percent; and foundation contributions, 8.4 percent. Contributions increased by 7.4 percent for the average independent institution and rose 9.4 percent for public institutions. For the second year in a row, the public institutions received the largest share (52 percent or $855 million) of corporate gifts. In the mid-1970s, private higher education received twice the amount of corporate gifts as public institutions.

Endowment and earnings

The financial gifts to colleges and universities are important for the revenue they generate when (and if) they become part of an institution's endowment. For most of the 1980s, the return on these investments for America's wealthiest institutions was in double digits. For 1988-89, the return rate was 13.9 percent; in 1989-90, the rate was 9.6 percent, the lowest in a decade (Jenkins 1991). Over the past 12 years, the purchasing power of the endowment funds has increased an average of 6.4 percent annually, which compares favorably with the Consumer Price Index of 5.8 percent. Thus, the investors have protected the purchasing power of the funds from the erosion of inflation. Unfortunately, the 1989-90 return rate did not do as well as the S&P 500 stock index of 16.5 percent (Jenkins 1991). These declining rates for colleges and universities also are responsible for a decrease in the spending rate of endowment earnings.

As earnings decline, a smaller percentage are expended, indicating that a greater portion is retained to expand the endowment. The total value of the endowments of the 367 institutions willing to report was $60.1 billion. Ten independent universities and the University of Texas system had endowments of $1 billion or more; Harvard led the list with $4.653 billion. Twenty-eight institutions, all with $400 million or more endowments, had 55.1 percent of the total endowments reported.

Revenue Needs

Revenues not only determine costs, but certain kinds of revenues generate costs. An example is the situation in which a public appropriation or a gift for a new building does not include funds for contract supervision during the construction process. Another example is the beneficent legislature which appropriates several millions of dollars to college and university libraries for book purchases but does not provide funds for the temporary help needed to complete the ordering process and shelving the new books (all of which needs to be accomplished in a single fiscal year). Most colleges and universities are appropriately grateful for the funds allocated for much needed projects, but find it hard to ask for a small amount to complete the projects. Sometimes poor planning and an absence of cost data from an institution leads to these omissions. Other times state law or the stipulations of the gift might prevent the expenditure of funds for these "implementing" purposes—another example of inflexibility with certain kinds of revenues.

Many other sources of revenues come from self-supporting services (housing, for example) but seldom move to the general fund. Most of these revenues—gifts designated for scholarships or sports ticket money to support nonrevenue sports —are restricted. But note that a benevolent president may take a portion of the receipts of sporting events and use it for academic purposes such as library books, faculty international travel, and so on. During the 1990-92 recession, many of these restricted and auxiliary sources of revenues have been studied carefully to see if they can help support the general operations of a college or university.

Another source of income that is problematic comes from the the sources designated "unrelated business income." Chartering cruises for alumni, profits from a bakery in the student union or from the sales of clothing items with the institutional logo on it are examples. The U.S. Internal Revenue Service and Congress have been working for years to develop a set of criteria that would tell colleges and universities which business activities would generate taxable income. The IRS now is considering designating television revenue from football games as taxable income. Current tax rates would determine the size of the loss to relevant institutions.

Finally, it must be pointed out that fund-raising activities and their foundations are playing an increasingly important role in the lives of colleges and universities. Public institutions, including community colleges, have become aware that they must increase gift revenue for both a margin of excellence and to support new programs. However, the cost of fund-raising and program management continuously needs to be reviewed to ensure that these activities are worth their cost of operation. An important test of planning and management arises when an institution decides it needs to mount a multi-year capital campaign. Adding staff and marketing specialists is not only important, but this staff must raise new revenues many times the cost of their salaries or the campaign will be a fizzle of unrealized grand expectations. Last is the fact that fund-raising during a recession might have certain disadvantages.

COSTS AND COST PRESSURES

Many factors are involved in generating costs and cost pressures. Constituent demands for more services and institutional demands for more resources stimulate cost pressures. The passage of time also increases costs as faculty, buildings, and equipment age and require increased resources to provide a minimum quality of services (Balderston 1974). Changing external conditions over which an institution has little control—economic, demographic, governmental, and postsecondary competitive factors—also stimulate costs. Inflation, recession, reduced birth rates and male college attendance rates, new government regulations, and other external variables demand expenditures unrelated to the educational functions of colleges and universities (Hauptman 1990).

Another source of cost pressures arise from an institution's quest for prestige and quality. Expanded aspirations unchecked by an understanding of costs and revenue sources are especially demanding. Expanded aspirations exist when an institution creates new programs, expands old ones, "stockpiles" faculty for these programs before enrollment growth, and takes other action to increase academic prestige and status. One might call this "risky planning," since the source of revenues to support this growth might not materialize. After expansion comes stabilization, which brings only modest increases of enrollments and revenues accompanied by rising expenditures (Baldridge 1974).

Adjusting to little growth, no growth, or recessionary cutbacks might only dampen cost pressures, not reestablish a new balance between revenues and expenditures. Reduced revenues might pressure a stable institution to restrict enrollment; that action might be followed by two-year institutions wishing to become colleges that offer bachelor's degrees. In states in which enrollment demand is increasing and public institutions are beginning to restrict enrollment, new private institutions might begin to emerge or branch campuses of out-of-state institutions appear to serve the surplus student demand.

Institutions that need students (and revenues) will take a variety of steps. The decisions to increase financial aid to students and expand the number being funded by allocating a greater share of general revenue for this purpose to aid recruitment might represent what Balderston calls a "conscientious overcommitment." Similarly, public institutions that enroll students beyond the number the state will subsidize might be fulfilling an important part of their mission but will create a demand for more funds across the board. One should note that accepting students without public subsidy will reduce instructional costs per full-time equivalent student and also probably reduce the quality of teaching and learning if the policy is continued for any period of time. Increasing revenues and costs of instruction might be appropriate if other institutional resources are being used efficiently and quality needs to be improved.

These and other factors stimulate cost pressures; they will be examined in this section. In the next section, the management and control of costs will be considered.

Cost Pressures from Unmet Needs

A universe of cost pressures arise from the unmet needs of various groups in and outside of higher education. These pressures include current and potential clientele groups, mandates from external sources, the demands (internal and external) for new programs or for enhancement of existing programs, and the suggestions of funding sources. When the pressures stimulate action, they increase expenditures and without more revenues raise the costs of higher education. Cost pressures—some persisting for many years—make strong demands on current institutional budgets and future budget requests.

External sources like governments, foundations, industry, alumni, benefactors, parents, and clients of programs provided by colleges and universities make demands for services and frequently offer resources in exchange. If the services demanded cost more than the resources provided, then some way must be found to bring them into balance. In response, the services demanded could be cut back, the payment or subsidy offered might be increased, existing resources could be reallocated from ongoing programs, or revenues might be increased from another source. The alternatives available are given such weight as the politics and self-interest of the institution seem to justify. For example, a public institution might elect to continue to admit students, even though they would not be funded under a state budget formula which limits the enrollment to be subsidized.

In some instances, external sources mandate programs or services and fail to adequately, fully, or even partially fund the mandates. State and federal government demands based on new social policy oftentimes fall in this category—such as affirmative action programs and implementation of new health and safety standards. Another demand, often a contract requirement, comes from some foundations and government funding sources who will not pay all or most overhead costs for projects they want completed. In other cases, they restrict the amount of overhead to exclude such elements as computer services or purchasing reference books. In these instances, the offer of resources for some services is made on a "take it or leave it" basis and, if accepted, the institution must fund part of the cost of the project from revenues designated for instruction or other purposes.

Inflation is a key factor in increasing costs. It is especially difficult to "fund" when the economy is stagnant and state revenues are declining or not growing. When revenues cannot keep up with inflation, attempts usually are made to raise tuition and fees; unfortunately, this action can reduce or flatten enrollment in some institutions, further reducing revenues and increasing the unit cost of instruction. Responding in these circumstances to the demands for new programs to fulfill unmet needs is especially difficult or nearly impossible.

"Mandated" Cost Increases

Mandated increases in costs arise from changing economic conditions, threats to financial solvency or profitability, and changes in governmental social policy. Stagnating or declining economic conditions reduce tax collections and funds for both private and public higher education. Worsening economic conditions reduce the discretionary income that students and their families need to pay tuition. In such conditions, both public and private institutions often attempt to raise tuition to make up for the expected decline in revenues. The alternative to the preceding chain of events is for institutions to postpone salary increases and/or cut programs every time the economy or enrollments dip. Strategic planning is a means to anticipate and manage the dips in the economic and demographic cycles (Morrison, Renfro, and Boucher 1984; Cope 1987). However, more than good intentions are needed to make planning work properly and usefully, as one anonymous reviewer reported.

Mandated increases affecting faculty and staff costs are many and substantial: social security charges, retirement programs, health insurance, workers compensation premiums, and salary increases resulting from minimum wage laws or collective bargaining. Institutional administrators who find they do not have enough funds to pay competitive salaries to hire staff and faculty at the skill levels needed find the market is demanding that they raise salaries. Colleges and universities in metropolitan areas face stiff wage competition from the federal government, the public school systems, and the private sector. In a state like Florida, many of the growing community colleges find that they cannot pay high-enough starting salaries for faculty with master's degrees to compete with the salaries paid beginning public school teachers with bachelor's degrees.

A biennial survey of 1989 retirement and insurance benefits by TIAA-CREF indicates that fringe benefits make up 21.1 percent of the payroll for the average college and university employer (*Business Officer* 1991, p. 12). Both larger and comprehensive institutions had higher rates, as did those in the Mid-Atlantic region. Rising health insurance costs are a significant example of a competitive or mandated cost pressure.

Institutions have found little relief for a wide variety of other cost increases; they don't have the ability to substitute other less costly goods or services, for example. Postage increases, travel charges, property insurance, and utilities have all increased in cost due to changes in technology, work load, and the availability of raw materials such as oil and gasoline. Although such cost increases are not clearly "mandates," they are virtually unavoidable. In the short run, most colleges and universities have little opportunity to change technologies or services to improve their costs.

Another set of costs which appear to be unavoidable are those resulting from natural disasters and their equivalent. The former include earthquakes, tornadoes, ice and snowstorms, and floods. The second category of disasters is illustrated by such tragic events as accidents, suicides, and the murder of students on or near campus. The result of the latter is that counseling and security programs of all kinds must be enhanced, lighting improved on campus, emergency telephones installed, and additional staff hired to prevent reoccurrence of such terrible events. Other critical events are fires, power outages (which damage sensitive equipment), student riots, and single-minded destruction of art work and library books. Insurance, which itself is becoming more costly, can cover some—but not all—of the losses from these events.

Another mandate-like expenditure is the payment that public and private institutions make to local governments and public service organizations. The need and justification for these payments is that nonprofit institutions pay no taxes but do generate a demand for services from police and fire departments, water and sanitation facilities, hospitals, and emergency medical services. The classic example is a city's need to buy an aerial-ladder fire truck after a university builds a nine-story residence hall, social science building, or bell tower. A Midwestern university in this situation donated land and funds for the construction of the fire house and the purchase of the ladder truck; the city then paid the salaries and benefits of the employees who staffed the facility 24 hours a day.

Similarly, a large college or university in a small town might stimulate a need for a nearby hospital to operate fully staffed prenatal, maternity, and pediatrics units, plus treatment facilities for terminal illnesses like cancer and AIDS. The university might have to help solicit gifts to enlarge a hospital and then annually conduct voluntary giving drives to raise funds to support facility operation.

Payments in lieu of taxes to municipalities are rising as local governments try to find more revenues. In 1990, Harvard is reported to have added $100,000 to its already $1 million annual contribution to the city of Cambridge, Mass. (*Business Officer* 1991). The same report indicated that Yale earlier had agreed to pay New Haven, Conn., "more than $2 million over the next five years for fire services and street improvements" (p. 15). Such other cities as Evanston, Ill., and Pittsburgh have attempted or are considering a levy of taxes on university students or research grants and some properties, because the higher education institutions in their cities do not pay taxes for the services they receive. In an even more unusual situation in 1991, the federal government's Environmental Protection Agency asked 13 colleges and universities in South Carolina to join with 100 companies and governmental units to pay the $10 million cost of cleaning up a hazardous waste site.

Another mandate-like expenditure is the payment that public and private institutions make to local governments and public service organizations.

Another special cost situation with few alternatives involves universities that have medical schools. Medical schools that operate their own teaching hospitals provide a variety of medical services to various groups. Various pressures exist to maintain minimum patient charges in order to obtain patients on whom medical students can learn their profession. Many medical services are very costly and require the hospital to seek as much reimbursement as possible from the patients, insurance firms, or government agencies (which pay for indigent patients).

When government does not offer a minimal reimbursement for indigent patients, the university medical school and its hospital can't do much except to raise the charges to those who can pay, which eventually means everyone with health insurance! University hospitals that provide this public service—needing patients, rarely can restrict the choice of patients to treat. Incidentally, university medical centers established to provide services for students now are finding that students without health insurance are leaving their schools with unpaid medical debts. Either the university and the doctors must be willing to absorb these debts, or they must require students to enroll with health insurance (Collison 1989).

Administrative Costs

Administrative costs have been rising as the number of administrative and academic support personnel has increased (Grassmuck 1990). Administrators might have increased as much as 60 percent between 1975 and 1985, a period in which faculty increased by 6 percent. This same trend can be found in the research sector of universities as reported below.

One analysis of this growth suggests that three sets of conditions explains it: regulation and micromanagement; consensus management; and expansion of administrative entrepreneurism ("The Lattice and the Ratchet" 1990). The first category focuses on the requirements of those external to the colleges and universities who audit and inspect and who demand reports of activities and plans. Administrative staff are necessary to respond specifically to the external regulators. As greater statewide coordination, regulation, and governance has emerged since 1960, public institutions have found it necessary to increase the staff who work with state and system officials. In many institutions, it was found necessary to create an equal or greater number of staff positions to match the state staff and the work load it generated.

The second category focuses on the need to spend greater amounts of time and staff on consultation among administrators in order to ensure that all appropriate "interests"—internal and external—are represented in the decision-making process of colleges and universities. Consensus management requires a lot of time, energy, and input from many sources. Consultation has expanded as more faculty committees have been created to help govern institutions; democracy also has its costs.

The third category suggests that staff costs continue to rise as the better-qualified staff delivers better services, develops expertise, and corners the market (like faculty) in their specialty area. These conditions lead to competition among the experts, hiring of more staff, expanded services, additional higher salaries—in other words, the ratchet effect. The analysis suggests that as faculty have increasingly lessened their ties to the institution for which they work, the role of the support staff has grown in importance. (The presumption that faculty at one time were much more involved in university governance and administration ought to be tested, just as these explanations deserve verification studies.)

Administrative salaries are a small share of current institutional costs, but it has risen. According to a national survey of administrative compensation published in the March 1991 issue of *Business Officer*, salaries rose by 5.4 percent, somewhat ahead of 4.7 percent inflation in 1990; this might have been a compensatory increase from the effects of inflation in 1989. The previous year, inflation was 5.1 percent and salary increases were 4.5 percent. Public institutions had larger administrative salary increases in 1990 than private institutions. The median salaries of chief business officers varied by the degree level of the institution and its budget size.

The ability of higher education institutions to pay a median salary that keeps up with inflation is an important achievement; whether that rate of increase extends throughout the administrative hierarchy was not reported. Attempts to keep salary increases at least equal to inflation is a cost pressure, even if meritorious in its intent.

The increase in the minimum wage set by federal law reveals the difficulties resulting from a well-intentioned public policy. In 1990, the minimum hourly wage moved from $3.35 to $3.80; on April 1, 1991, it increased to $4.25. The 1989 law that set these rates also created a lower training wage for teenagers; in 1991, it increased from $3.35 to $3.62.

Colleges and universities hire semi-skilled adult workers at hourly rates or what rates the market requires for service jobs; it also pays students hourly wages for shelving books in libraries. However, if the budgets of institutions do not increase to cover the additional cost of the higher minimum wages, then fewer students are hired by the library. That's what happened at many colleges and universities in 1990; the number of students employed in the library at Florida State University decreased by 25 percent that year for these reasons. Similarly, some students working at fast-food restaurants and other service businesses faced the prospect of unemployment after 1991. The 1991 increase also might stimulate a ratchet effect in which higher paid hourly workers demand a proportionate increase in their hourly wages. The ripple effect of these mandated wage increases has a number of undesirable consequences even when we agree that the minimum wage is not a living wage and should be increased.

Faculty Costs and Characteristics
Faculty salary costs
The faculty salary costs of an institution vary according to the degree qualifications, academic rank, and seniority of its faculty. An institution with a large number of faculty who hold doctoral degrees and are full professors with 20-25 years of service will be expensive. According to the March/April 1991 issue of *Academe*, the primary source for national faculty salary data, the all-ranks average faculty compensation for 1990-91 was between $35,480 and $49,320. The all-institution average was $43,720, which rose 5.4 percent over 1989-90, although the increase fell below the rate of inflation for the first time in many years.

Salaries at four-year public institutions increased at a lesser rate than those at private or church-related institutions. The expectations for 1991-92 and later are grim because many states have had to cut back funds for higher education and many other services during the recession. The pressures to find salary funds had escalated in both public and private institutions when inflation recently was above 5 percent and insurance and other costs, which continue to rise, absorb a larger share of salaries.

Many cost pressures are related to faculty salaries: inflation, competitiveness with the salaries of other professions, faculty shortages, higher salaries for new faculty, demands for reduced work loads, increased cost of fringe benefits, and others, such as the employment of a spouse. Obvious pressures exist to raise salaries to attract faculty and to keep those already employed. Because faculty salaries are such a large portion of the current operating expenditures of institutions, these cost pressures have significant effects on current and future budgets and instructional costs.

Inflation. The impact of inflation in the 1970s, when faculty salaries were left behind, often is used to explain the increase in salaries, institutional budgets, and tuition in the 1980s. "Despite recent actions to narrow the gap, faculty salaries today on average are still about 9 percent lower than in 1971-72" (Hexter 1990, p. 1; Hauptman 1990). The onset of the 1990-1992 national recession will further restrict the ability of institutions to close the 1970s inflation gap; its growth will create more cost/revenue pressures. What happens when the recession ends and state tax collections and private giving rise is dependent on the robustness of the recovery, inflationary pressures, and the public's willingness to provide greater funds.

Some have had an earlier experience with this problem. A 1960s salary policy at Indiana University, a large multi-campus research institution, was labeled "catch up and keep up." The need to regain the purchasing power of faculty and staff salaries lost during the recessions of the early 1960s led to a variety of stratagems to increase appropriations. At this particular institution, the catch-up salary policy was designed to increase the salary ranking of the institution among its peers in the Big Ten. However, when all institutions in the league attempted to increase their salaries at the same time (because revenues were increasing at the end of the recession), the rankings did not change, even though everybody became better off!

The state legislature wanted to see the ranking improve, because members were told that would be the consequence of a large catch-up appropriation; obviously, some legislators were unhappy. Cost pressures did lead to risk-taking so that the university could remain competitive. Stanford is a university that strives to keep salaries at one or two percentage points above inflation to remain top ranked and competitive nationally and worldwide.

Are faculty overpaid? The president of York College of Pennsylvania, Robert V. Isoue, asserts that faculty are underworked, not overpaid (*Higher Education Costs* 1988, p. 234). He draws a comparison between underpaid high school teachers with multiple responsibilities (Russell 1931, p. 23) and the large majority of faculty members who are better paid, but do not conduct any research and teach only nine hours. Increasingly, the level of faculty workload is seen as a cost pressure; it is discussed later in this text.

Retirement. One of the prime factors that might affect instructional costs in the near future is faculty retirement. In the next 25 years, as many as 40 percent of faculty (and administrators) in most two- and four-year institutions could retire; some say the exit will be at a steady pace (Bowen and Sousa 1989). However, many academic administrators are expecting a surge of retirements by 1994. The state university system of California estimates that it will need 8,000 to 9,500 replacement faculty and an additional 6,000 to cover enrollment increases by 2002 (Jewett 1989).

Another uncertainty about faculty retirement trends is the question of what will happen when the age cap requiring retirement is removed for faculty in 1994. In that year—unless Congress acts to the contrary—there will no longer be a mandatory retirement age for faculty. Currently, the average retirement age is a fraction over 65. If faculty retire later, the salary costs should increase; administrators wonder whether they need to create better incentives for early retirement. Unfortunately, such action might accelerate the anticipated increase in retirements among the faculty who began teaching in the 1960s—creating unwanted shortages of experienced faculty. An added complication to this complex situation: Will one of the side effects of the 1990-1992 recession be that 65-year-old faculty members postpone retirement until economic conditions and current salaries begin to rise across the board again? Remember that some retirement programs take the last five years of salary to compute the monthly retirement benefit.

Retirements mean that the fundamental cost structure of faculty could change significantly by the year 2010. Faculty costs could fall as more faculty are hired at the assistant rank; or, salary costs could increase as institutions bid for a relatively small pool of graduates to replace the retirees. By 1997, about four candidates will be available for every five openings in the arts and sciences (Bowen and Sosa). One of the primary factors that could be holding down faculty costs now is the increasing use of part-time faculty. The 1970s saw part-timers grow from 22 percent to about 34 percent of total faculty (Frances 1990); that trend might have reached 38 percent or higher by 1990 (Leslie 1991). It is much higher in community/junior colleges.

Salary fairness and equity issues

Two faculty salary fairness issues that generate budget requests and therefore pressure the costs of instruction are salary compression and salary inversion. The latter occurs when a department must pay a higher salary to a new faculty member than it pays the experienced faculty already employed. This occurrence lowers morale and leads to demands for better salaries and more equitable workloads. Salary inversion occurs because recruiting new faculty responds to the pressures of competitive market/salary conditions, the availability of alternative employment opportunities, increases in productivity or expertise, inflation, or special local factors such as geographic area cost of living). Institutions might adopt a "catch up and keep up" budget and fund-raising strategy to cope with this condition. They can pressure their state legislatures and private benefactors to increase institutional revenues to cope with this problem just to keep their best teachers and researchers.

Another kind of salary issue is the compression of rates that result when faculty and staff receive similar salaries or when salary varies little by rank among faculty or staff. Similarly, salary levels between administrators and faculty can become closer when pay for the former is held steady and pay for the faculty is increased. Steady-state funding or actual reductions in funding over several years are often the root cause of these conditions; whether they constitute a problem depends on faculty and staff perception. In a capitalistic society in which money talks, undifferentiated salaries by skill level and seniority can fail to perform as incentives for achievement or a continuation of high-quality work. The interim president of the University of South Carolina stated in March 1991 that his institution annually set aside as much as $200,000 to adjust salaries found to be caught in the conversion-inversion tangle.

One of the potential cost items regarding fair faculty salaries is what might be called "the price of salary sex equity." The potential consequences can be estimated from a simple calculation. Multiplying the 1982 estimate that a $1,000-3,000 salary discrepancy per female faculty member exists (Koch 1982) by the U.S. Department of Education's 1985 estimate of 128,063 full-time female instructional faculty produces an estimate of a very large potential future funding obligation: $128,063,000 to $384,189,000.

The size of the salary disparity for women in higher education seems to be growing. In 1972-73, the average salary of female full-time faculty was 83 percent of the average male faculty salary. By 1990, females were averaging 75 percent (National Center for Education Statistics 1990; Hexter 1990). In addition to the back pay for the salary differences, institutions could face large legal fees and fines if discrimination is proved. One difficult aspect of this issue is that few legislatures separately fund sex equity. In the public institutions, the funds for equity salary adjustments often must come from the total funds appropriated by the state for faculty salaries or salary increases. The demand for salary equity funding is a definite cost pressure; it has been around for more than 20 years.

Another development that might turn into a faculty salary cost pressure is the growing differences of average salaries by discipline (Hexter 1990). Salaries already vary by degree level of institution, rank of faculty, gender, race and ethnicity, region, and control (public, private, and church). Hexter reported that salary increases have been greater by roughly one percentage point for engineering and computer science faculty than other fields and about two points over education faculty (p. 5).

The pressure to equalize salaries across disciplines does not seem to have an active voice in 1991. Faculty labor unions often demand equal pay for equal work; they want the external market forces muted inside the institutions when they see higher salaries set for certain disciplines such as business finance or computer science.

Salary costs from benefit programs

Some fringe benefits generate costs even when they have no direct cost. An example is the personnel policy that permits new parents to take unpaid leave for three to six months after the birth or adoption of a child. The cost arises from the search and support for a teaching replacement when faculty colleagues can't absorb the increased instructional load. Finding an appropriate and qualified temporary instructor for a short period is not easy in many cities and towns. Qualified people in the high-cost disciplines such as physics, chemistry, computer science, engineering, and accounting just might not be available. It might be necessary to bring qualified faculty out of retirement or even to employ lesser qualified individuals. In the high-cost programs, even the temporary instructors might be more costly than the faculty who are taking leave.

Another side to this situation: The vacant position often is filled with part-time faculty who are paid at rates less than those of full-time instructors. If qualified part-timers are available, this arrangement actually might reduce the cost of instruction; what it does for the quality of instruction and adherence to the basic curriculum is another matter. Clearly, these are important trade-offs that arise from a benefit program that many find desirable.

A further development of this policy that can generate instructional costs has emerged; it involves a college permitting a faculty member to reduce his or her teaching load while still being paid a full-time wage. Carol Kleiman, a national newspaper columnist who focuses on labor matters, wrote that Albright, Baldwin-Wallace, Beloit, Hood, Knox, and Macalester colleges had implemented either paid or unpaid family leaves; fathers, as well as mother employees, were included at many of these institutions (1991). A college would need added resources to cover the increased instructional costs from the reduced teaching loads if other faculty couldn't cover the added work load and temporary teachers had to be found.

It should be noted that these very humane family-leave policies benefit the colleges by encouraging faculty to stay on rather than taking leave or resigning. The policy might help reduce the turnover of faculty and also help women to build a tenure-earning career at their colleges. The policies do have costs and do generate cost pressures among institutions that compete for faculty; however, their long-range benefits might outweigh the initial costs. The plan bears watching.

Fringe benefits

According to a 1990 TIAA-CREF fringe-benefits survey of 634 institutions, retirement and insurance plans cost 21.1 percent of college and university payrolls. The average amount per employee was $6,206; the median $4,635. The average percentages varied by type of institution (the highest was public comprehensive universities at 24.5); by region (Mid-Atlantic was highest, the Southwest and South were lowest); by size (larger institutions spent more); and by control (public institutions spent more than private).

No two-year colleges were included in the TIAA-CREF survey. These percentages cover an entire institutional payroll and would be substantially different for separate groups like faculty, technical, and clerical employees. The percentages of benefit deductions vary by groups within an institution, especially when an important part of the benefits are in flat dollar amounts for all employees. Then the lower paid employees could have a larger percentage of their paychecks devoted to fixed-dollar benefit charges, for example. A large public university with such a system (set by the state) could have 28 percent insurance costs for faculty and 34 percent for clerical and service employees for the same kinds of coverage.

The TIAA-CREF survey reported that legally mandated benefit expenditures averaged 6.6 percent of payroll. Social security taxes were the largest mandatory charge and accounted for 5.9 percent of total payroll. Administrators were most likely to pay the maximum charge for social security: 7.6 percent. Workers' compensation programs averaged 0.7 percent and unemployment compensation costs were 0.1 percent. Fringe benefits are the cost category with the highest rate of growth (Frances 1990, p. 13). However, it is the social security taxes, Frances says, that drive the cost increases. It should be noted that not all higher education institutions participate in the social security system.

Pension-retirement plans averaged 8.0 percent of payroll; they could be 15-18 percent of the faculty payroll. Insurance benefit expenditures averaged 6.5 percent of payroll, with 6.1 percentage points designated for health insurance. Long-term disability income insurance averaged 0.3 percent of payroll; travel accident insurance was 0.1 percent. Many different kinds of plans exist—some with coverage defined narrowly (for full-time, low-risk employees, for example) or more inclusively, and with several different kinds of coverage. Collective bargaining contracts may determine the kinds and costs of many benefit packages.

The rising cost of health insurance is placing a strain on fringe benefit budgets. These costs are rising so consistently that the 28 public community colleges of Florida had asked again in 1991-1992 for separate appropriations exclusively for health insurance. In the profit sector, businesses are reporting annual increases of 20 percent in their health insurance costs (Kramon 1991). An insurance consulting firm reports that the health costs per employee have escalated from $1,942 in 1987 to $2,646 in 1989, a 36 percent increase (Roush 1991). Driving up costs are the billions of health care bills remaining unpaid to doctors and hospitals that subsequently are shifted to taxpayers and people with health insurance.

In Florida, the unpaid bills are estimated to total $1.6 billion; 18 percent (2.2 million people) of the population is without health insurance (Troxler 1991). The Florida Legislature is attempting to pass measures to control this situation. A large number of changes in health insurance are being adopted nationally, including charging more for those at risk (smokers and overweight people, for example); rates also are being differentiated according to the extensiveness of the coverage desired. These and many other approaches are being tried in the attempt to hold down health care insurance costs, which are not yet contained!

The rising cost of health insurance is placing a strain on fringe benefit budgets.

In states in which the salary and benefits of public colleges and universities are controlled by government, individual institutions might have little say about the rising cost of health insurance. If handicapped by poor state management and stable appropriations, the rising costs of health insurance and retirement are likely to become a drain on the funds allocated for salaries or salary increases, when the latter exist.

Work load and productivity

A former president of two public universities (one on the East Coast, the other in the upper Midwest) suggests that the reduction of teaching load per faculty member is one of the most serious causes of rising costs in higher education. A current president of a large public university in the South says there is little evidence that productivity of faculty increases as the teaching load is reduced. In a related vein, faculty are working less as the academic year has shortened—a reduction of one month since the 1960s (Cheney 1990). The consequence of reducing the teaching work load is the pressure to hire more faculty or use an increasing number of part-time/ adjunct faculty or graduate teaching assistants.

Several surveys of faculty about their work load have been conducted over the years. One of the latest is the 1988 National Survey of Postsecondary Faculty sponsored by the National Center for Education Statistics. In 1990, Fairweather,

Hendrickson, and Russell prepared a special report for NCES describing the activities and work load of faculty reported in the 1988 survey. The data reported here are taken from their paper.

Using the data from both two-year and four-year institutions, the survey revealed that the average faculty work week in 1988 was 53 hours. Forty-six hours (87 percent) occurred at the home institution, four hours (7 percent) were in other paid activities, and three hours (6 percent) were in unpaid service activities. Faculty in research and public doctoral institutions reported above-average work weeks; faculty in private comprehensive institutions and in public two-year colleges showed work weeks below the all-institution average (pp. 2-4). However, the survey revealed that community college faculty spent more time teaching and teaching more students than any other group. Generally, faculty at the research and doctoral-granting institutions spent less time teaching than the comprehensive and liberal arts groups. The differences reflect the missions of these institutions.

Faculty in the senior ranks or those who were tenured worked more than the all-institutional average work week (pp. 2-5). Teaching activities took above-average time for faculty in business, education, the humanities, and natural sciences. Other significant disciplinary differences included:

> *Faculty in education, the fine arts, and the humanities spent a less than average percentage of their time on research activities. Faculty in education were the only members who spent a higher than average percentage of their time on administration and on service* (pp. 2-5).

These self-reported sample data depict a faculty that works much more than a 40-hour week. Such data present a significantly different picture than one shown in the rousing book *ProfScam* by Charles Sykes (1988).

The matter of faculty work load is one of the most troubling in all of higher education. Institutional and national data exist in fragments, and no reliable standard definitions are used. Great differences exist between programs and disciplines within and between institutions; to protect the autonomy and independence of the academic units that make decisions about the most effective use of their human resources, there is little enthusiasm for collecting work-load data. The latter is true even though a number of states have work-load laws of one kind or another that demand institutions to make good-faith efforts to compile such data.

Within academe a clear feeling exists that spending time and money to perfect a data collection system will only consume resources that could be better used for the primary purposes of teaching, research, and public service. Also, it is believed that the data collected from such a system will not improve the efficiency or effectiveness of institutional operations. However, parents, taxpayers, and legislators increasingly are clamoring for institutions to carefully examine their work-load policies and to confront the issue of who should teach undergraduates and how much time the average faculty member should spend on teaching. These complaints seem lodged more about teaching in large public institutions that tend to have larger classes than in private colleges and universities, although none are immune to these complaints. It should be realized that smaller classes increase the cost of instruction.

State work-load laws or administrative rules specify, on average, the number of hours faculty should devote to instruction. Florida has a 12-hour law for university faculty, but the law permits administrators to make exceptions for professional activities that are judged equivalent to regular classroom instruction (Florida Statutes 240.243). The equivalencies include directed individual study, thesis and dissertation supervision, supervision of interns, and other special kinds of instructional arrangements. Teaching large classes and preparation time for new courses also can be designated equivalents. The larger and more research-oriented universities require more and different exceptions to the 12-hour law. Additional equivalents have been approved for research and service, some administration, and student advising. Faculty in the law and medical schools are exempted from the requirements of the Florida statute.

A proposal in the Florida Senate to remove almost all of the exemptions was considered and defeated in spring 1991. The stimulus for the proposal was that more than one-third of the faculty at the two primary research universities were teaching only six hours, while some of the other universities had only 10 to 15 percent of their faculty teaching a similarly reduced work load; here also the differences were based on institutional missions. The legislative analysis of this proposal, which would also raise the minimum contact hours to 15, indicated that these "under-loaded" research faculty would have to increase their instructional activities by 150 percent.

In committee debate, the Senate sponsor asserted that 500 fewer positions were being used by the universities for instruction than had been funded by the legislature; he estimated that some $60 million appropriated for instruction was not being used for that purpose. The chancellor of the university system responded by pointing out that more than 1,200 research positions were still being funded that had been authorized back in the 1960s. The ostensible purpose of the legislative proposal was to "increase student access to courses required for graduation and enable students to graduate sooner, thus reducing their educational expenses." Although this proposal had little chance of passing the 1991 legislative session (and didn't), it dealt with issues that have been raised in many states over the past five years. No one expects these issues to go away; a lingering recession only can stimulate interest in proposals to increase faculty work load and thereby reduce the cost of instruction.

The central point to be pondered from the preceding data and information is whether instructional costs are being pushed up by faculty who have reduced teaching loads; unfortunately, there is no good answer. There are isolated reports that some institutions are hiring replacement faculty before they are needed and not requiring these individuals to teach at all. The latter is said to be one of many ways administrators are coping with the shortage of new faculty expected in the late 1990s. During an economic recession, the pressures are even greater to hire part-time faculty—and where available, teaching assistants—to hold down costs. In public institutions, administrators are pressured not to fill authorized faculty positions, but to take the funds and hire adjunct faculty and graduate students. This strategy also allows more and smaller teaching sections in undergraduate courses. Whether this practice is beneficial to students remains to be documented; however, it is believed to help control salary and instructional costs.

Instructional Costs

The largest component of instructional costs is faculty salaries and benefits, considered previously. Other instructional costs include libraries, computers, television and media equipment, laboratories and scientific instruments, and such specialized facilities as theaters, music halls, art studios, and gymnasiums. However, it is the push for additional programs (majors), new graduate degree subjects, new technical specialities, and new courses to accompany the new programs which drives up instructional costs. Some of the pressures for new programs arise from the possibility of serving a new market, of faculty gaining greater independence, of pioneering the development of new fields, and of adding to an institution's prestige. During the 1990-92 recession, larger classes might have become the norm and instructional costs decreased; the educational consequences of this change might not be known.

Instructional systems

One of the newer terms describing television teaching is distance learning. Through the use of telephone transmission lines, cable television, and satellite relays, it now is possible to schedule educational programming 24 hours a day. Many states are building these instructional systems for kindergarten through high school students. Some states, like Indiana, used everything but satellites in 1967 to provide professional continuing education for lawyers, nurses returning to practice, and other professionals. Instruction for engineering students in Florida is being offered using the methods of distance learning.

The use of two-way audio with video communication permits interaction between an instructor and students. The technology permits one instructor to teach two or three classes simultaneously. If a camera is available at each learning site, the instructor can rotate weekly among the sites to physically (rather than electronically) interact with different classes. Elaborate course planning, preparing attractive visual aids, and avoiding "talking heads" are required to present electronic instruction. Great care must be taken if a quality video production is to be made for subsequent broadcast. Even with these electronic wonders, some kind of staff assistance is required at the additional learning sites; if they are faculty or higher paid teaching assistants, then the cost of instruction per student credit hour might not decline at all.

The distance-learning technology requires substantial capital investment to cover the cost of constructing satellite receivers and sending equipment, for example. Usually a network must be established, costs determined for operating the system, and backup arrangements made for the times when the power goes off, equipment malfunctions, or other interruptions occur to the scheduled transmission. Both administrators and coordinators as well as instructors and technical staff are needed for a basic distance-learning system. All of these systems and their costs often become supplementary to the traditional systems of instruction.

At some point, evaluations will have to be made to determine if this form of instruction generates the same (or a greater) level of learning as the traditional in-class model and whether it is worth the added cost of the telecommunications technology and the additional support staff. Presently, colleges and universities are being pressured to adopt electronic instructional systems to expand access to place-bound students. In the past, it was hoped that the emerging electronic teaching technology could replace faculty; instead, it was found that the technology was used to supplement the faculty members' efforts and thus raised the costs of instruction. Whether learning was enhanced from these technological augmentations has not been demonstrated to the satisfaction of most faculty.

Libraries. The electronic revolution has taken libraries by storm in the last five years. First came large national computerized data base utilities for bibliographic research, then placement of the same data on compact disks. Next came the national and state system data bases of college library books, then the addition of the journal indexes onto the book systems. The next information retrieval development will be to permit computer retrieval of the text of journal articles from either CD-ROM system or regional/national article data bases, when the copyright problems can be solved. The text of books would be likely to follow if their copyright problems could be worked out. Some text retrieval of journal articles already is available on CD-ROM. This portends the power to search an enormous number and variety of texts. The widespread use of electronic bibliographic files appears to have increased the use of inter-library loans to obtain copies of journal articles unavailable in some college libraries.

These developments are an example of using technology to stimulate greater use of library materials; but in some cases, this has added duplicate costs. (For example, both the hard copy of the journal indexes must be subscribed to because the electronic data bases on compact disks are only leased, not purchased so they can be updated quarterly.) In addition to the rising costs of new technology, the costs of serial publications such as scientific journals have increased enormously—some as much as 600 percent over the last three years.

Many major universities (Berkeley, Texas, North Carolina, SUNY Albany) have been reviewing and cutting their journal subscriptions not only to balance their budgets, but also to try to restore some of the funds taken from the book budget that were required to pay the journal price increases. In all, the relatively low salaries paid to librarians has helped hold down library costs. Libraries often take about 6 percent of an institution's budget; older and larger institutions would spend more. New or additional library space probably will be needed by the year 2000 as well as a larger investment in electronic data bases and computer terminals to access the new journals that will exist only in computer data bases. All of the preceding are growing cost pressures.

Complex Enrollment Issues

A minimum enrollment often is specified before a new public institution, campus, center, or program can be created. The presumption is that a specific minimum enrollment justifies the higher administrative costs, because the small enrollments aren't economically efficient. The idea that size determines an efficient operation is an old one in economics and business; it also seems to apply to higher education. A minimum size of 500 to 1,200 full-time equivalent students often is suggested in state master plans. However, much research remains to be completed before generalizable criteria exist to create new institutions and programs.

Declining enrollment on a campus leads to concern for the survival of an institution. It is the pressure of increasing costs due to declining revenues that begins the concern for all manner of cost control strategies, discussed in the next section. Decreases in enrollment initially increase costs per unit of instruction. Generally, an increase in enrollment will reduce overall unit costs. However, educational costs might not decline if expenditures rise significantly to obtain the new enrollment, as for marketing and recruiting, financial aid, counseling and advising, records and registration, retention programs, and student services. One of the consequences of decreasing enrollment is that fewer students remain among whom to spread the fixed costs such as the cost of operating buildings, libraries, and administration. If no other sources cover these costs, then tuition must be increased for this purpose. That's usually what is done by state universities (Hauptman 1990).

Concerns about the costs related directly to services provided to students leads to some very complex issues. Questions have been raised during research about the causes of increases in tuition. One of these issues is whether declining revenues and rising costs (for instruction, for example) drove up tuition or whether tuition was increased to permit greater expenditures—maybe for computers or more financial aid for students. The first assumption is that the prices for goods and services purchased for higher education have increased faster than inflation. The second idea asserts that institutions have been spending money on new types of products and services, or purchasing more of them.

Kirshstein and others summarize the preceding and other explanations (1990). They then report their research results using national aggregate data and their own simulation model to test the workings of these two explanations (pp. 81-84). The research indicated that both sets of factors were operating on both public and private institutions in the period 1980-1985; however, rising tuition revenues did not significantly stimulate additional expenditures in the period 1975-1980. The 1980-1985 period saw expanded and expensive efforts to recruit a declining pool of high school graduates, especially by the private institutions which primarily depend upon tuition revenues.

Research Expenses
The results from a survey of university department heads in 1985 revealed that 72 percent believed a lack of equipment was preventing critical experiments. The need to establish a research infrastructure to attract scientists, graduate students, technical support staff, and funders (revenue providers) generates cost pressures on universities. For those who have the resources, keeping up with the rising costs and holding together research teams while funding agencies make decisions about continuing project support add to research costs. Institutions without reserves to cover these gaps in external funding risk the loss of valuable support staff.

Research and support staff

The need for talented researchers, research apprentices (graduate students), support staff, and others connected with research activities continues to grow. Scientists, mathematicians, and engineers in universities require competitive salaries and benefits to remain in their home institutions; their highly technical skills enable them to readily find high-quality employment in government laboratories, research and development firms, and for-profit corporations with a need for scientific analysis. Similarly, the need for large stipends to attract and hold graduate students in science is very important.

In recent years, fewer Americans have been attracted to doctoral programs in science; the remaining need for research apprentices has been filled with foreign students to the point at which these individuals constitute one-third to one-half (or more) of graduate science enrollment. The decline of federal research fellowships and the forecasted oversupply of scientists in the 1970s are offered as reasons for the current enrollment situation. The future need for more scientists is leading universities now to "stockpile" scientific faculty: College enrollments nationwide are expected to increase after 1995, and the faculty hired in the 1960s are expected to retire in the 1990s. Clearly, stockpiling is expensive and workable, but only available to those with the funds.

Support staff. A key component in the cost of research is the support staff, referred to as research support personnel by Hensley in his 1985 testimony before a task force of the U.S. House Committee on Science and Technology (*University Research Infrastructure* 1986). Although the exact size of this group is not known, Hensley estimated it to exceed 500,000 people. Included in this large group are 12 functional classes: grant and contract officers, program development officers, business managers, clerical personnel, academic officers, research center staff, animal caretakers, laboratory personnel, shop personnel, medical personnel, agricultural extension and experimental station staff, and others. The first half-dozen classes have a strong administrative focus but are necessary to keep the research enterprise going. People in these classes are involved in research activities at various times: some during the pre-award stage, some during the conduct of the research, and others throughout the entire process of sponsored research. People who hold these positions are part of the research infrastructure.

Not included are the student assistants or research investigators who carry out the essential research activity. Hensley reports that 75 percent of all those working in research are support staff; faculty researchers constitute the remaining 25 percent. It should be noted that many—if not most—of these staff people are employed only as long as contracts and grants are received to pay their salaries. However, research directors do everything possible to keep together a research team; the pressure sometimes leads to bad financial practices.

Research equipment and facilities

The need for better research equipment and better funding for such equipment was reported in detail in a 1985 report by the American Association of Universities, *Financing and Managing University Research Equipment* (reprinted in *University Research Infrastructure* 1986). The report summarized the need with these conclusions from an earlier survey:

1. Of the university department heads surveyed, 72 percent reported that lack of equipment was preventing critical experiments.
2. Universities' inventories of scientific equipment showed that 20 percent was obsolete and no longer used in research.
3. Of all instrument systems in use in research, 22 percent were more than 10 years old.
4. Only 52 percent of instruments in use were reported to be in excellent working condition.
5. 49 percent rated the quality of instrument-support services (machine shop, electronics shop, etc.) as insufficient or nonexistent (p. 462).

A key cost pressure has been reducing federal funds for leasing or purchasing equipment; a 78 percent decline (in constant dollars) occurred during 1966-1983. (However, the federal government was still the largest funder of equipment—54 percent—in use in universities during 1982-1983.) Federal funding has been an important source to cover the rising cost of the sophisticated tools and facilities for scientific research in American higher education. Of the $20 billion spent on civilian research and development, about $6 billion is invested in university research (*University Research Infrastructure* 1986, p. 6).

Cost reimbursement

The overhead cost-reimbursement rates authorized by the federal government for research grants and contracts vary to the extent an institution can justify the costs permitted to be recovered. A survey of 30 universities with large research expenditures showed different rates between public and private institutions: "The average indirect recovery rate of private universities was 63.6 percent in 1986, as against an average of 42.8 percent for the public university campuses" (Balderston 1990, p. 48). The private universities believe it would be disastrous for them if they didn't recover a maximum amount of indirect costs.

For the public institutions, the recovery rates might be low because state government provides so much of the basic funding. Often the state governments demand that portions of the reimbursed overhead funds are returned to them because of their support for the public institutions. As a result, public university research administrators often believe they are denied the funds to which they are entitled. The belief is widespread among all university research administrators that the federal government does not pay a full share of an institution's indirect costs.

Faculty researchers often complain that their grant proposals are handicapped by high cost-recovery rates because they increase the total cost of the grant project. They request that their institutions absorb more of the indirect costs, which would have the effect of shifting such costs to non-research units. Faculty in private universities with the highest indirect cost rates feel they are losing out in the competition for research projects, because their total project budget is too high.

During the past decade, the cost-reimbursement standards of the federal government have changed; to researchers and administrators, this has led to the systematic underestimation of university needs. In 1985, one of President Reagan's science advisers, Dr. Bernadine Healy, testified before a Congressional committee that facilities-use allowance reimbursements "are based on an average useful life of 50 years for a university laboratory. The actual average useful life of a laboratory is probably about 20-25 years, as it is for industrial laboratories.

The belief is widespread among all university research administrators that the federal government does not pay a full share of an institution's indirect costs.

As for research equipment, in addition to having unrealistically long amortization periods—fifteen years, in contrast to the actual six to eight—the government also micromanages the purchase of new equipment" (*University Research Infrastructure* 1986, p. 13).

Cost Studies

Cost pressures can be anticipated by carefully analyzing the factors in the environment most likely to impact an institution. Reports of inflation, economic stagnation and decline, new federal laws, the possibility of postal increases, desegregation court decisions about Southern university systems, and many other developments will demand an assessment of their potential impact on higher education. One way that college and university administrators could respond to these reports is that each one could assume responsibility for surveying the external environment for future changes. However, a strategic planning analysis would require a coordination of these efforts just to identify cost pressures that would require institutional planning and management. Enrollment changes also must be monitored along with the emergence of competing institutions to determine if the student market has altered due to external or internal conditions.

Tracking enrollment and cost changes within an institution is another strategy. It requires a great attention to detail and systematic study; organizations like NACUBO and NCHEMS can provide guidance in such activities. Unfortunately, one of the first services to be discontinued when revenues decline is the analysis of the use of resources within an institution. These times are the ones most in need of good cost analysis, especially if little planning or forecasting has been done to anticipate a possible decline in revenues. When coupled with a focus on managing and controlling costs, these studies of both external and internal factors help an institution shape its future.

MANAGING AND CONTROLLING COSTS

The costs of higher education are a concern to many people. A variety of external forces attempt to restrict the rise in costs. Some, like state governments, force reductions in costs, even when not specifically targeting them. States do this by reducing revenues or mandating a productivity increase and then implementing it by arbitrarily deducting a percentage of appropriated funds. States may attempt to manage and control institutional costs in a number of arbitrary ways.

Managing costs in higher education is both art and science. A knowledge of budgeting (see Meisinger Jr. and Dubeck 1984) and financial management in higher education is helpful. A brief description of activities involved in financial management of colleges and universities has been prepared by Hyatt and Santiago (1986). It contains a good description of the data and information needed to make useful financial decisions. A skillful analysis of the core concepts of financial and cost management have been presented in *Managing Money in Higher Education: A Guide to the Financial Process and Effective Participation Within It* (Vandament 1989). The author's view of managing and controlling costs is:

> *Approaches to reducing costs sometimes involve the rationing of resources, such as supplies or staff; in this case ongoing activities are accomplished without change in the basic method of delivery. Other approaches involve significant changes in the way services are provided, such as consolidation of fragmented support operations or contracting for services with outside agents. Effective financial management typically includes a never-ending search for ways to reduce costs while maintaining quality in the organization's services* (p. 11).

The view that the effort to control costs is a continuing activity which must be accompanied by a concern with quality establishes an appropriate purpose for managing costs in higher education. By implication—and specifically stated by Vandament—efficiency is not a primary purpose of financial management; providing quality services through the wise use of resources is an appropriate goal. That view is congenial with the purpose of this monograph.

In this section the issues important to keeping costs and benefits in balance as cost pressures mount are considered. In addition, the management of costs and expenditures will be considered under various kinds of financial stress, such as the short and longer term financial emergencies resulting from a decline of revenues and/or students. It is assumed here that the costs of goods and services to be purchased by an institution are known elements. It also is assumed that it is necessary to know the cost of institutional activities and programs if costs are to be managed.

Furthermore, almost all studies about financial management indicate a need to know what is most valued in an institution; the implication is for clear statements of mission, goals, priorities, and some agreement about the outputs desired from the use of public resources. Although many institutions lack such specificity or a plan to implement it, the search for it should give meaning to the management of their scarce resources. Coping with scarcity in the pursuit of quality academic outcomes (rather than just budget cuts) can be the focus of any program to effectively manage the institutional costs of higher education.

Revenues to Cover Costs

Raising revenues to cover costs is a goal. When this is not achievable, expenditures must decline. Sometimes costs must be increased to raise more revenue. Revenues which lag behind inflation might control costs or even lower them, but educational quality also might suffer. Increasing revenues from various sources should be worth the cost of the activity required to raise more funds. Whenever possible, revenues should be increased according to the mission, role, and scope of each institution.

One of the more pernicious suggestions for raising revenue in the short run is to delay remission of insurance and retirement premiums so that interest can be earned for the institution instead of for the employees. This proposal involves great risk when an institution wants to maximize interest income and invests premiums in unsecured stocks, bonds, and commercial notes. The problem is that what can go up in value also can come down unexpectedly. Many states have laws that restrict or prevent implementation of such poor ideas. However, in difficult economic times, many old and bad ideas often materialize.

A major point about fund-raising is that accepting just any gift without estimating the secondary costs could prove troublesome over time. It still is true that a gift of an astronomical observatory to a college can lead to the creation of a department of astronomy. The gift would be acceptable if it is integral to the mission of the institution. Unsolicited gifts or special appropriations from friendly legislators raise the same issues.

Many institutions receive gifts of land, buildings, businesses (a circus, for example), and art work. It is especially important to estimate the costs of keeping and operating buildings before they are accepted. Such troublesome items as asbestos insulation, lead-based paint, old wiring, lead-soldered plumbing, an ancient heating and cooling system, and termite and rodent infestations all reduce the value of a building. The price of fixing up the building might be higher than the price for which the institution (or its foundation) feasibly could sell the property. This situation has come to the attention of state legislators who see these "hidden" costs as an unnecessary drain on facility and future operating budgets. In many ways it is very hard for a college or university to turn down a gift of an attractive small museum packed with prehistoric artifacts. But the security and utility bills could mount rapidly, especially if the museum is located 125 miles from the main campus of a university. An endowment gift must be obtained to cover the costs of operating the museum, preferably before the museum is accepted by the institution. The same holds true for the gift of the papers and memorabilia of a distinguished alumnus; who will pay for the cataloging, security, and guidance for the use of these materials? One should carefully inspect a gift horse.

Increasing enrollment for revenues

A concern with rising costs and slow-growing revenues leads many institutions to consider recruiting more students as a revenue source. The basic thought is that a few more students in each class would not be an unreasonable increase in work load for existing faculty and the tuition revenue (and state subsidy for public institutions) would offset some existing costs.

The impact of a student increase would depend upon the size of an institution and whether the increase would be phased in over a number of years or only a few. The generation of cost-free revenue always is problematic. For example, there is no way to bar students from electing high-cost programs or programs that do not earn enough resources to cover their costs. Thus, it is possible that a marginal increase in students will further unbalance a budget.

Usually, when an institution has unused capacity, adding students to programs that break even (in costs and revenues) is a benefit. However, additional costs of support services might tax an institution; an increase in part-time students raises these expenditures. Costs might rise in the admissions, registration, and advising offices as a result of growth in student numbers. Library services and materials might have to be expanded to accommodate enrollment growth. Student services such as counseling, health care, recreation, housing, and entertainment also might increase costs, although separate fees could offset some of the rise in these student service costs. It should be remembered that student tuition pays only a portion of the total cost of higher education.

The matter of tuition as a viable revenue source is important, although it may be kept low to encourage access to college. In the public sector, several states are raising the out-of-state tuition rates to cover the full cost of education. The indexing of tuition to the amount of increase in state revenues, to the rise in the cost of living, or to a fixed percentage of the cost of education shows a movement to try to make tuition a more dependable source of revenue. The effect of these increases on enrollment might be to direct more students to the public community colleges. Maximizing revenues from tuition might be possible only for the wealthiest institutions.

A number of colleges are spending funds to better market their institutions as a means to increase enrollment and revenues. Those that can afford it also fix up their campuses to make them more attractive places (*Higher Education Costs* 1988). Some institutions increase their intercollegiate athletic budgets to develop winning teams and to generate favorable publicity and more revenues. The strategies are important, but they all have costs.

Balancing Costs and Benefits

The plans, programs, and activities to keep costs on the continuing agenda of institutional administrators are important elements of a cost management strategy. They should be undertaken *before* a financial emergency arises; they might moderate the effects of uncontrollable external events and with good fortune, they might keep an institution solvent and functioning at a satisfactory level of quality.

One approach to finding and solving institutional financial problems before they get out of control is illustrated by the activities begun at Johns Hopkins University in 1989 (Fuchsberg 1989). Johns Hopkins is financially sound with a budget surplus, but its eight degree-granting divisions do not fare equally well. Two academic divisions, Arts and Sciences and the Peabody Conservatory of Music, showed "chronic unfunded balances." After officials projected the unfunded balances for these and other units (such as the main library and radio station) for the next five years, a broad range of operating cuts and revenue enhancements were implemented to bring balance to the finances of all units. However, the report indicated that it took a year of agonizing discussion to agree upon an appropriate course of action. In some ways, the early detection of emergent financial problems and development of workable solutions might be more difficult than trying to confront a financial emergency, but the long-range benefits should be greater.

Cost-cutting programs

Cost-cutting programs may be directed to particular services or activities. Energy conservation would require that an individual in each building or area be responsible for turning off lights each evening and seeing that the thermostats were set as high as possible in hot weather and as low as possible during cold weather. Weatherproofing windows and creating double-entry doors to contain cool air in summer and warm air in winter also are important. Unplugging water coolers, turning off automatic door openers (except those for the handicapped), and shutting off escalators also might be tried as ways to save energy and its costs. However, such adjustments must be monitored and reinstalled repeatedly to maintain effectiveness and produce a savings. A realistic and annual assessment of the cost of such control efforts needs to be carried out over several years to ensure that the costs do not exceed the benefits.

Cost-cutting programs sometimes emerge as part of an institution's effort to improve the quality of its services. The "Total Quality Management" program at the Oregon State University is one such example (McMillen 1991, pp. A27-8). By studying the financial and business services at the university, administrators and clients attempted to improve them by reducing the time to complete work. Changes in the work processes were expected to save time, improve quality, and reduce costs.

It was reported that Oregon spends about $50,000 a year to develop and adopt the plans necessary to make the needed improvements under TQM. The initial results were that the time to complete construction projects dropped from 195 to 150 days. The 23 percent decrease in time, with some reduction in costs, made the improved space more readily available to faculty, staff, and students.

NACUBO has reported that about 25 colleges have adopted TQM, including Pennsylvania's Edinboro University. In the four years since it has implemented the program, Edinboro reports a savings estimated at close to $1 million. An in-depth review of TQM is being prepared by Ellen Earle Chaffee as a future report of ASHE-ERIC.

Objections to transferring the TQM methods to the academic programs of an institution have been raised. Because universities are not businesses, many faculty members are seriously skeptical about applying a business-oriented strategy to the work of higher education (McMillen). One of the central ideas of TQM is to pay attention to the complaints and needs of clients—in other words, the students. Some faculty find this approach important. It might become very important if students decide not to enroll or to drop out because their needs seem to take a back seat to the needs of the faculty and administrators. TQM seems to be the latest strategy after quality control circles to gain the attention of both profit and nonprofit organizations.

Cost reductions

An emphasis on reducing costs while maintaining quality requires a search for lower cost alternatives to the usual ways of providing services. The forming of consortia of institutions to obtain discounts for large orders of supplies, equipment, and even library books is an example of such arrangements.

Relationships with industry often are seen to have a positive benefit for the research, development, and training activities of colleges and universities. Contributions of state-of-the-art equipment or price reductions for such equipment through educational discounts can be significant benefits. Minimum-cost maintenance agreements for expensive and complex research equipment also may be negotiated directly with equipment manufacturers.

The shared use of equipment and facilities is a significant strategy for acquiring access to items that otherwise would be prohibitively expensive if purchased. Florida State University's supercomputer contract with the U.S. Department of Energy (DOE gets priority use of the equipment 60 percent of the time) and Ohio State University's statewide supercomputer network proposal are examples of shared use.

Facilities for training such as field camps, laboratories, and telescopes can be shared with other colleges, special interest groups, government agencies, and even business and industry. Colleges and universities also might seek special arrangements to use national laboratories, computer facilities, and special library collections administered by the federal and state governments. Even with a modest user fee, the latter might expand greatly the educational resources available to a college or university. Large municipal and state libraries often provide services without charge to students and faculty of colleges in their service area. Small colleges might find the electronic bibliographic search programs of municipal libraries far superior to their own indexes and card catalogs. The central strategy here is the search for ways to gain access to valued resources without acquiring the resources.

Another similar approach here is the contracting for services. In this manner, expertise is rented or leased rather than developed within the institution. The need for elevator repair service can be satisfied either by institutional staff or by a private business in the area. The number of elevators and their general condition often indicates the need for these kinds of services. A similar situation arises from the need to repair office equipment, computers, printers, and communications equipment. Where highly unique scientific equipment must be designed, built, and maintained by an institution, it is more common to find technicians and artisans (glassblowers, for example) on the staff of a large college or university.

One of the important consequences of contracting for services is that costs (salary charges) might not rise as fast as those in institutions where across-the-board salary increments can increase service costs beyond the average charged by businesses. Of course, contracting outside for services could inhibit development of the skills unique to the needs of a particular institution.

Tactics for controlling costs

Ever since the 1970s and the Arab oil embargo that drove up
oil prices and utility costs, lists have appeared to suggest
actions that colleges can use to manage costs—representing
potential solutions to financial problems (Ginsberg 1982).
It is easy to forget that many institutions suffer similar financial
problems, but that the solutions they choose depend upon
their local history, tradition, culture, and views about the
future.

Suggestions on these lists range across a full set of options.
For example: To finance the operation of the residence halls,
lower the room rates to attract more students; raise the rates
when student demand for on-campus living is high; lease the
halls to a private service company; or sell the halls to a hotel
or apartment management firm. The solution chosen should
meet the needs of the institution and include consideration
of both the optimal financial arrangement *and* the contribution of residence-hall living to the college experience.
Because most of the suggestions on these lists were conceived
during financial emergencies, they tend to remain in the standard repertoire of management responses to financial problems. The suggestions are examples of areas in which financial
alternatives may be considered to increase revenues or to control or reduce costs.

One of the most important areas in which to control costs
is that which absorbs the greatest share of the academic budget: instruction. It is considered in a following section as a
special cost category.

Managing cost pressures

Most colleges and universities—even the wealthiest in the
United States—must cope with the cost pressures detailed
in the previous section of this monograph. Many must con-
stantly make adjustments in tuition charges and program quality just to keep revenues and expenditures in balance. Public
institutions, depending heavily on the health of state economies, find they must make do with whatever comes their
way. In response to living in a constant state of need for additional revenues, all institutions have tried a wide variety of
strategies to cope with their perceived adversity. These actions
are believed necessary even though they might have undesirable consequences.

For example, across-the-board budget cuts often are used

to contain costs at the level of insufficient revenues. Employing this strategy too often is thought to lead to "rising mediocrity" (Jaschik 1989). Leaving vacant faculty positions unfilled—regardless of the program from which they originate—is another way to contain costs and jeopardize program quality. The high-quality programs are as likely to lose faculty as weak programs—or maybe more so.

After a financial squeeze persists for a few years, the need crystallizes to examine programs to determine if any should be cut back or eliminated. This is seen as a strategy to generate funds for new programs or to enhance old ones. This kind of major surgery in a college or university is very traumatic and might take several years to accomplish. One always should be prepared for faculty and staff to deny the need for even a judicious paring of programs; they would rather see a substantial reduction of administrators, student service staff, medical services, and support staff. These and other strategies most often receive keen attention when an institution finds itself in financial difficulty.

What is required is a continuing series of cost studies . . . to determine if the administrative services . . . are being provided efficiently and effectively.

Administration

Controlling administrative costs is a major challenge. Belief is widespread that many administrative costs are mandated or at least required if an institution wants to compete for students, research grants, and service contracts and to provide a healthy, safe, and fair work place. What is required is a continuing series of cost studies, analogous to academic program reviews, to determine if the administrative services already justified as absolutely necessary are being provided efficiently and effectively (see Brown 1989). Proceeding in this direction without succumbing to the latest management fad is another challenge, as Allen and Chaffee indicate (1981).

A recent guide to administrative cost studies is *Tough Choices* (1990), based on a recognizable linear model of planning and administration. Over the years, the National Center for Higher Education Management Systems has developed a variety of approaches to cost studies, although most have focused on instructional costs. A major element of many cost studies comprises examining salary data and comparing this data across similar institutions. The American Association of University Professors annually publishes such data for faculty in its journal *Academe*, and the *Chronicle of Higher Education* publishes average data for many kinds of administrative positions.

Administrative salaries

Much has been written and discussed in the daily press about the salaries that "retiring" administrators take with them when they return to their faculty or become faculty members. Managing these costs is a real challenge. One method of holding down administrative costs is to clearly designate the portion of an academic administrator's salary for this function. For example, when a faculty member becomes a department chair or part-time administrator, the salary increase for these duties clearly should be labeled a supplement. The increase should last only as long as the person holds the job. A reasonable supplement for a department chair should be a significant benefit ranging from $1,500 to $3,000. A chair guaranteed a half-time summer appointment as the principal supplement should retain this benefit only while functioning as chair.

In a similar vein, a full-time administrator—whether recruited from within or outside the institution—should receive downward salary adjustments when he or she assumes a faculty position. If the administrator was on a 12-month appointment, then he or she should remain on the payroll for that duration for one or two transition years. The first reduction after the transition period should be a return to a 9- or 10-month salary—in other words, to 75 or 83 percent of the former 12-month salary; summer appointment would then be subject to the same requirements governing faculty colleagues.

The second part of the reduction should include a return to a salary level equal to the pay received by the average or above-average faculty member of equal seniority at the institution. Comparability could be determined by noting the salary of a regular faculty member at the 75th percentile of all salaries in an appropriate academic department or division; adjustments could be made to the 67th or 85th percentile depending upon the quality of the "retiring" administrator's work. An institution's policy for this kind of reduction also might set a floor (as well as a ceiling) for the size of the decrease or permit the reduction to occur over a period of three years to avoid undue hardship. The objective here is to determine fairly the salary of a "retired" administrator in relation to the salaries of the faculty to be joined. Given the great variety of pay and perquisites for administrators, any reduction plan needs to reflect local conditions.

Instructional Costs

Instructional costs include expenditures for programs, faculty, academic support operations, libraries, and other related activities. Instructional costs vary according to the disciplines of the teaching faculty, their seniority in a teaching career, class size, and the extent to which classroom instruction is augmented by laboratories, field work, and special teaching equipment such as computers. Continuing expansion of the use of computers is considered one of the factors driving up instructional and other costs.

Instructional systems

One of the important variables affecting instructional costs is the mix of educational experiences designed for students—large classes, small classes, tutorials, and self-instruction. A further refinement is designing instructional systems so that they accommodate the various learning styles of students (Kolodny 1991, p. A44).

The tutorial between a student and an experienced professor still tends to be the most expensive form of instruction which, of course, explains the high cost of doctoral programs. The large lecture section staffed with teaching assistants or adjunct instructors can be the least expensive. The extent to which any of these methods serves desired educational purposes—rather than costs—should be the reason for selecting one or another of them. However, when resources are declining, classes commonly become larger and choices become fewer.

Individualizing courses according to a variety of learning styles is an appropriate educational goal. However, the cost of that effort, if it requires more than asking a faculty member to change his or her method of instruction, could be very large. However, an educational goal to recruit more minorities and women for careers in science might be an opportunity to begin developing more individualized courses of instruction. The costs to accomplish this more valuable goal may be rated as more worthy of support than simply adding greater instructional variety to the educational experience of students.

A focus on learning outcomes—the learning objectives that

students need to master—also could legitimize the costs of developing more individualized learning experiences. The fundamental issue remains, however, whether scarce resources should be used for this purpose or for some other (Will some other valued learning experiences or other valued programs be relinquished if the learning styles of students are emphasized?). This is an example in which the availability of educational goals and priorities could guide budget and expenditure decisions; of course, if such policy information arises only from a highly decentralized system, it might be too particular to be helpful across an entire institution.

It is possible to deliberately create a mixture of educational experiences while balancing their costs. Bowen and Douglas illustrate with economic analysis an approach to using existing resources to create a variety of teaching and learning experiences for students (1973). The key to undertaking this analysis is the availability of information about the goals of individual courses: which ones are designed principally to transmit information and concepts, which focus more on creating an appreciation of the subject matter, and which require the student to learn and demonstrate a unique set of behavioral skills. The first category of courses may be taught in larger classes, the second in smaller classes, and the third might require small classes or individual instruction. Depending on the needs of an institution or the needs of the schools and departments within it, other categories can be created to maximize the variety of learning experiences available to students without increasing expenditures.

Another area with clear cost implications that is related to instructional systems is the use of computers, software, video tapes, films, and other media. The issue of licensing under copyright law can make many of these materials more expensive than necessary. For example, if a state government's department of education has the authority to purchase such materials for use throughout education, it might be able to offer substantial savings on copyrighted materials. Such materials can be obtained on loan, copies made for use, or programs transmitted over cable or by satellite for recording by educational users. In some states, even a central budget is provided for acquiring materials for postsecondary education. Similarly, colleges located near a large institution that houses a film library might be permitted to borrow materials for a nominal fee. The focus is (or should be) on obtaining access at a reduced fee, rather than purchase for acquisition of these various materials.

Full- and part-time faculty and classes. Class size policies—the minimum- and maximum-size classes permitted at an institution—significantly affect costs. Such policies might cause a sudden rise in instructional costs if full-time faculty are hired at the beginning of a new program when classes are small. It might be better to hire part-time faculty until some critical mass of students are enrolled. Similarly, a surge in enrollments might be met by temporarily employing part-time faculty to prevent class sizes from rising excessively. Hiring part-timers also would permit the administration to study the factors leading to the enrollment increase, thus avoiding a premature permanent commitment to more full-time faculty with their higher and continuing costs.

An expanded instructional program might have to be carried by the existing faculty in larger classes until it is clear whether the expanded enrollment is a temporary phenomenon or a more permanent change. The nature of the changes in enrollment must be studied carefully. If real growth is reflected by new students entering the institution rather than by current students selecting a more acceptable major, then part-time faculty can be replaced by a full-time instructor.

After a successful program is institutionalized and the enrollment patterns become fairly predictable (although shifting still can be evident), a policy may be followed. Perhaps one full-time faculty member could be added whenever a specified minimum number of student credit hours are added; for example: 300, the equivalent of a four-course work load averaging 25 students each enrolled in a three-credit course.

Very early commitment of new faculty positions to a new program that doesn't raise enough revenue to cover direct instructional costs will become a drain on other revenue-producing programs at the institution. A similar situation emerges when faculty or administrators promise to create a new program "which won't cost anything because all of the needed faculty and support resources are already on hand." That might be true initially if the program has unused capacity and low faculty work loads. But without growth, other programs will have to help out. If funds are available, as when a chief academic officer creates a venture capital fund each year, then new programs could be supported in part with such funds (Vandament 1989). Clearly, institutions must carefully manage the costs emerging from new programs in which the primary purpose is to attract new students and revenues to an institution.

Programs

Programs often are synonymous with departments or divisions (the latter term is used in smaller two-year and four-year institutions), although more than one program may exist in a department; interdepartmental degree programs also might exist as well. Programs most often refer to instructional units or degree curricula, but also include service activities such as counseling, fund-raising, security, and many others. At the institutional, system, or state level, programs might refer to all instructional expenses and include most other departmental costs such as the research, development, and service activities not separately funded.

Programs costs may be reviewed each year at budget time, every five years during program reviews, at start-up time, when programs are merged, or when a new program emerges from an old program (computer science from mathematics, for example). Many times program costs are not estimated; the omission contributes to the poor management of costs. At other times, surrogates for costs are used, such as the number of FTE students when funding or budget allocation formulas require specific quantities to generate a faculty position (see Tucker 1986). In such cases, the faculty positions then are multiplied times an average institutional salary to estimate faculty costs.

Proposals for new programs sometimes contain estimates of desired expenditures for their early life—for the first three years, for example. New programs begun with existing faculty and available resources often contain no projections of future costs. This omission might be deliberate based on the often erroneous assumption that only existing resources will be used in the program. In other instances, the omission is based on the decision to see whether sufficient enrollment (a cost surrogate) materializes to warrant continuing the new program. When coupled with a set of criteria to make a continuation-termination decision, the costs of new programs might be adequately controlled through the review process.

Programs created to meet a perceived demand in society sometimes begin before a sufficient enrollment demand exists; these programs might have to be "unstarted" and tried later under more favorable conditions. Periodic needs assessments in local areas, regions, states, and national scopes help determine whether enrollment demand is likely to emerge for a new program.

Break-even analysis. The estimates of future costs are needed for both new and continuing programs in order to determine which programs generate revenues beyond their costs, which ones have reached a break-even point, and those that require support from other programs. Special attention to the subsidized programs is necessary to estimate when (and if) they will become self-sufficient—that is, when costs and revenues will balance. From this analysis, enrollment growth targets need to be established so that progress indicators are widely known and understood; failure to meet the growth targets after a few years should place a program's existence in jeopardy. Clearly, some programs (classical languages, for example) may be considered necessary in a particular kind of institution; such programs are not self-sufficient and rarely break even. Vandament uses a nine-cell table with a variety of criteria to determine how each program should be classified (1989).

Sometimes the departments and schools that generate a surplus of revenues over costs complain that they are required to subsidize the departments that don't break even. This is one of the more difficult situations institutional administrators face and in large part is due to decisions about curriculum and degree programs and the average work load of faculty. The need for a unified curriculum almost always will involve programs that produce revenues and other programs that are weak in this regard. Program enrollments also can be responsive to swings of interest in particular majors. Pre-law can give way to a preference for pre-medicine; investigative journalism can become popular after the press uncovers a national scandal; education might be avoided because teacher wages are too low; science might be considered too demanding except when Earth Day and ecology become popular topics. Shifting choices create varying patterns of curricular costs over time, and the trick is to know why student preferences change and whether the changes are short-, medium- or long-term.

Institutions with decentralized operating budgets often find that some schools generate surpluses, some break even, and others generate losses. A business school might generate a surplus from both careful management and enrollment demand of students. An arts and science college might find it difficult to break even because of the many departments and great variety of subjects needed for the lower-division foundation programs of freshmen and sophomores. Of course, the specialities of arts and science faculty might lead to very small classes at the upper-division and graduate levels of instruction. The latter drive up instructional costs and might comprise such limited attractiveness to ordinary students that class enrollments are likely to be too small indefinitely. Clearly, small classes and unique subjects must be justified academically to claim a subsidy from other courses or programs.

It should be clear that not every program or course will be able to pay its own way. Retaining uneconomical programs should be an educational decision; such a decision should be attained with a full understanding of the extent to which such programs prevent others from reaching their academic potential. It's hard to muster the courage to terminate a program that doesn't live up to expectations. One way to approach this problem is to periodically conduct program reviews or evaluations (Micek 1980).

Program reviews. The systematic review of an ongoing program can contain a specific examination of direct salary costs and other expenses of the program. The review should assess whether the expenditures are reasonable for particular kinds of programs such as those without laboratories and those with small classes. The number of student credit hours generated also will be needed to estimate the revenue of the program. Then, the ratio of costs to revenues should be determined to classify a program as one that provides revenues or requires subsidies or whether it is breaking even financially.

The point of the review using ratios essentially is to raise questions about the educational quality of the programs. For example, the departments generating surplus revenues should be assessed to determine whether they are rigorous enough in their academic requirements as well as whether they're attractive. The departments that generate deficits should be examined to determine if they are too difficult or restrictive, currently unattractive to students, or not a part of the central curricular emphasis of the institution. Those that are breaking even need to be examined for both sets of concerns. The ultimate judgment is whether the costs are appropriate for generating the desired quality of educational program and whether poor-quality programs should continue or be allotted additional revenues.

A wide-open program review involving outside subject-matter experts often will result in a recommendation for more faculty and staff and other resources. In fact, a study of the program reviews of the nine-campus State University System of Florida for an early five-year period revealed that all programs needed more resources. The programs were judged on the basis of their need for an increase in quality. This clearly indicates the need for program priorities, since not enough resources exist for all programs.

In the process of the total program review, cost information usually represents only one kind of evaluative information. The cost information is given greater weight during difficult financial times, and this presents a problem. The program review originally was conceived as a systematic means leading to program improvement. As enrollment and financial problems demanded attention in the 1980s, the program review came to be seen in many places as the basis for eliminating programs. In some institutions or state university systems, collective bargaining agreements required that a program be abolished before faculty could be laid off or terminated.

The potential threat of a faculty layoff resulting from analyzing program review data has spawned several problems, including the centralization and analysis of data collection. Nonetheless, the systematic program review with clear and public criteria for making decisions about program continuation—whether or not such programs are uneconomical—might be in the best interest of an institution. In other words, cost alone should not be the primary reason for terminating a program. Instead, some criteria, such as the extent to which the program contributes to the central mission of the institution, is more important.

Faculty. The acquisition of a new faculty position and a new person to fill it entails a bundle of start-up costs including office space, furniture, typewriter or personal computer, and office equipment and other appropriate items. Many institutions have a room or building for new and used office furniture storage that could help meet the need. The appointment of a senior professor might require more costly office space and accouterments. Research faculty require a variety of facilities and equipment; scientific equipment can cost from $25,000 to $250,000, depending on the discipline and the experience of the researcher. Among the disciplines in which library materials are used for research, a faculty member's specialty might require adding a special collection of books and periodicals. Institutions should be prepared to supplement the library budget each time a new faculty position is created, but this rarely is done systematically.

Faculty salaries constitute the largest portion of direct instructional costs—that is, the portion of the budget necessary to pay instructors for their teaching activities. These costs usually vary by discipline, seniority, and type of institution. Compensating faculty includes offering a salary plus the fringe benefits of health insurance, retirement, and supplements.

The need to control insurance costs is very clear. In Florida, seven community colleges have formed a self-insurance consortium administered by Blue Cross-Blue Shield that has reduced rising health costs from 15 percent annually to below 8 percent. To be successful, these new and innovative approaches—which include health maintenance organizations—require broad participation and very careful management. Given the forecast of continuing and probably increasing health insurance costs, institutional and system officials will have to give more time to this expenditure category.

In the strictest sense, the costs of student assistants, technicians, and others needed to keep laboratories and equipment functioning are all part of the cost of instruction. An important administrative concern about the use of instructional facilities and equipment is that it must be available when it's needed and has to be fully utilized to realize its value. As satellite transmission, interactive video discs, and other teaching technology are utilized more widely, the equipment technicians could become as important as the teachers. In the past, teaching technologies have not replaced faculty but have only added costs to the process of teaching and learning. The 1990-92 recession surely will stimulate another round of experimentation with electronic substitutions for faculty instructors. We still need to know whether learning is enhanced through instructional technology.

Institutional Equipment

In purchasing equipment, whether for administrative, teaching, research, or service activities, an estimate of full costs is very important. Full costs include those related to renovating space to hold the equipment, shipping, installation, security, operation and maintenance, service contracts, technical support, insurance, utilities, and special supplies. If equipment is to be leased or purchased with borrowed funds, interest and service charges should be calculated, for they too are directly related costs.

The equipment data base is one of the more important information files to be created and maintained.

Furthermore, records of usage and depreciation charges must be maintained for research equipment that is to become eligible for funding under federal grants; usage allowances tend to be lower than depreciation over the estimated life of the equipment. It should be noted that different federal agencies apply varying interpretations to the regulations governing use and depreciation charges. For example, the allowable portion of rent or maintenance costs of a president's house is subject to interpretation, so early inquiry and thorough analysis are doubly essential.

The equipment data base is one of the more important information files to be created and maintained. In addition to the typical data about cost (including all cost categories), the records must include information about the length of actual useful life, repairs, and suitability for different programs and projects. This kind of data is needed to assist in the periodic study of institutional expenses to substantiate grant and contract overhead charges.

Sources of Financial Problems

How do colleges and universities get themselves into financial difficulty? "Conscientious overcommitment" (Balderston 1974), poor oversight and management, inadequate cost data, and lack of adaptability to changing external conditions (through poor strategic planning, for example) are some of the main sources of financial problems.

Upon taking office, a new college president found "that the budget had been balanced only through sales of property, fortuitous bequests, and delays of several months in paying bills" (Breckon 1989, p. B2). The first problem identified was the use of one-time or nonrecurring revenues to cover operating costs and liabilities. The second arrangement of neglecting to record expenses during the period when the services were received was a violation of Accounting 101 principles. Breckon explains that he fired 18 unneeded employees, sold staff cars, and took other actions to control costs and balance them with increasing revenues; he then gave the faculty a raise. This is one style of management and cost control with which most businesspeople, legislators, and trustees can identify in a very positive way.

Hiring too many full-time faculty and awarding too many 12-month contracts are other problems. Creating faculty positions whenever unused funds appear is another example. What is needed is some form of position control, which is a procedure to prevent creating positions without fully justifying and identifying recurring fiscal support. It involves controlling any vacant positions before they are filled, so that a faculty opening within a department may be assigned wherever it is needed most in the institution. Position control also involves closely monitoring new programs funded externally through development grants or contracts. This especially is important when it is uncertain from where the resources will originate when the grants expire in cases in which such programs will be institutionalized. The number of faculty and staff on short-term funds can be controlled by stipulating in the employment contract that appointment renewal is dependent upon the availability of funds and by clearly indicating that regular appointments are not automatically available to persons on "soft money" or one-time contracts.

A variety of other financial problems exist—such as the simple aging of faculty and buildings—that increase costs almost imperceptibly. As the budget requests rise each year, all activities must be thoroughly reviewed to determine which are the most essential to the central mission of the institution. Responding to this information in a timely fashion before a financial emergency arises is the job of higher education's administrators and managers. Perhaps better planning and institutional analysis would alert these officials to potential financial problems.

A number of indicators can alert administrators to the extent to which an institution is in or is headed for financial trouble (Mingle 1981). Some of the more obvious warning signs are:

1. A slow decline in students or an increase in empty dorm beds;
2. Holding admissions open until the day before classes

begin, even at open admissions institutions;
3. An exodus of senior faculty or excellent teachers;
4. Sending departmental budgets in December instead of on July 1 or at the beginning of the fiscal year;
5. Regularly missing cash discounts on accounts payable and delaying payment as long as possible;
6. Failing to give pay raises or cutting fringe benefits;
7. A high bankruptcy rate (more than 15 percent) on student loans;
8. Borrowing money to pay current operating expenses—beyond the need for temporary cash advances;
9. Postponing payday by a week or a month;
10. Selling property of any kind to obtain current funds;
11. Closing a building that has been declared unsafe because no funds are available to renovate it; and
12. Threats to regional accreditation.

In sum, many indications of financial problems exist. The top administrators or managers should agree on an appropriate set of indicators and incorporate these into an administrative MIS.

Managing Costs During Financial Emergencies
Institutions have little choice when they are confronted with financial emergencies: They must take certain actions if they are to survive. But all of these actions have secondary consequences—some of which might emerge only in later years. This section describes the strategies and tactics used in financial emergencies and some of the consequences of their implementation.

A temporary revenue shortfall, like a short-term recession, may be managed with four typical actions to reduce costs—plus a fifth action to transfer reserve funds to replace lost revenues. A multi-year decline in revenues resulting from a prolonged recession or a dip of the birth rate 18 years earlier would require more stringent adjustments and actions. Operating under a deficit for two or more years is courting disaster. The various strategies for coping with these financial situations are cumulative, although some—cleaning offices only every other day, for example—generate only a one-time cost saving. The strategies and tactics used widely will be described as shorter term and longer term approaches to managing costs.

It should be noted that publications such as the *Chronicle*

of Higher Education, the *New York Times*, and many other
newspapers as well as journals such as *Change* carry descrip-
tions about the various approaches institutions use to cope
with their financial difficulties.

Coping with short-term financial problems

Short-term financial emergencies bring forth a predictable
repertoire of responses to manage costs and declining
revenues. The first of these is the spending freeze, which
might extend to vacant positions, out-of-state travel, purchase
of equipment and library books, and any other relevant and
controllable expenditure. A variant on the freeze is indefinitely
postponing implementing new programs or construction projects. A freeze on faculty replacements or new positions might
stimulate the expanded use of part-time faculty when enrollment demand remains firm in particular programs.

A second tactic with strong future cost implications is postponing maintenance and reducing janitorial services such as
lawn mowing and window washing. Postponing maintenance
can allow a problem to develop or worsen, thus multiplying
the costs of repair and replacement. A third response might
be conserving resources: turning off lights and changing the
thermostat settings for heating and cooling, for example. It
also can include attempts to ration supplies and lower purchase prices by buying more generic goods and buying in
larger quantities to gain volume discounts. A fourth tactic
when revenues fall significantly is the across-the-board cut—
more recently referred to as "a policy for the equal sharing
of financial pain." The central objective of these four strategies
is to preserve as best as possible the regular services offered
by the institution, especially those which generate revenues.

A fifth category of action is to transfer uncommitted funds
from whatever source—some of which specifically might have
been created for emergencies—so that the most important
activities can be continued or enhanced. The principal sources
are general fund balances, nonrecurring revenues (revenues
from the sale of used equipment, for example), and discretionary funds. Many institutions have ample, separate, largely
discretionary budget accounts: funds for supplies, travel,
books, equipment, and (sometimes) salary increases. Addi-
tionally, funds are maintained for all of the institution's
unfilled positions or those soon to be vacated. The latter provide the savings from attrition of faculty and staff so often dis-

cussed as a means for reducing salary costs. Unfortunately, attrition might not reduce instructional costs if highly productive faculty exit the institution.

It should be clear that all uncommitted funds are ready targets to use in financial emergencies and often are treated as unlabled reserve funds. Many times, money for equipment or even for library books is not spent until the end of the fiscal year, so it may be used to cover a short-term financial emergency. These "contingency" funds could be transferred to departmental operating budgets to make up for lost revenues. When funds for instruction are still short—even after the transfers have taken place—elective courses could be canceled or simply not offered; the part-time faculty members who might have been used for these irregularly scheduled courses are left unhired.

Another response to a short-term emergency is to begin an effort to increase revenues through new academic programs, increased student recruiting, establishment of student retention programs, better government relations, expanded fund-raising, and so forth. These efforts are expected to boost the next fiscal year's budget. Although reducing programs is an action that might be considered at this stage, the legal complications and poor prospects for immediate savings usually prevent an attempt at partial implementation.

The general goal sought during the short-term financial emergency is to install spending reductions that impact as few employees as possible, so that roughly the same amount of instruction and services can be delivered. This goal might even lead to sending administrators to teach one or two classes a year. One hopes that these individuals, like part-time faculty, are qualified, current in their discipline, interested in students, and informed about the department's curriculum.

Budget reductions. If responses to financial emergencies are not carefully planned, the consequences can be a tangle of costs, dislocations, and conflicts that exceed any short-term benefits. For example, the fourth tactic—the across-the-board budget cut—often is seen as the most equitable way to confront a financial problem. Unfortunately, purveyors of that action fail to recognize that large departments are likely to have more budgetary flexibility than small units. Thus, the larger units might be able to give up some resources without affecting the level of service offered, whereas this would be nearly impossible within the small department. In addition, a "fair" or equal-percentage distribution of budgetary cuts fails to recognize the potential impact on high-priority programs—those which bring prestige, students, and external resources to the institution.

If funds set aside for matching certain types of grants and contracts are frozen or cut, then important losses of revenues could occur. These and other kinds of restrictions tend to discourage the best faculty, who then might be encouraged to leave the institution. If they are research faculty, they might take their research grants and graduate students with them.

Some faculty and administrators believe that the uniform percentage cut of all budgets has a beneficial effect in an emergency. They suggest that everyone believes that he or she is in the same predicament and must band together to make the best of a bad situation. The feeling of solidarity and belief in the institution, it is suggested, can even lead faculty and staff to accept pay cuts for one or two years to ensure that the institution becomes financially solvent again. These feelings contrast with those that result when some faculty and staff are told that their programs are not as worthy as others after program funding priorities have been set.

An alternative to uniform percentage cuts is designating particular expenditure categories for reduction: prohibiting long distance telephone calls or altogether removing telephones from faculty offices or desks, leaving an "outside" phone in the departmental office, for example. The latter action is designed to reduce the instrument rental charge as well as the cost of local and long distance calls. Implementing these options could negatively affect recruiting, service programs, and research efforts, especially if a faculty member has a computer and communications modem installed on his or her telephone for retrieving data and information.

Another problematic choice during a short-term financial situation is to take funds from the book budget of the main library. The funds might solve the immediate need but won't touch the underlying management issues of priorities and program retrenchment. In addition, a lack of regular expenditures would create "holes" in the library collection. Failing to purchase new books at the time of publication can be problematic: Because the press runs of academic monographs have become smaller over the years, they frequently are out of print only a year or so after publication—and thus later on are more expensive and perhaps more difficult to acquire.

Freezing expenditures. A freeze on spending is probably unavoidable in short-run emergencies. It is manageable if funds have been set aside (encumbered) to pay for purchases and contracts already negotiated. Without encumbered funds, responses to financial emergencies can be chaotic and followed by the costs of legal proceedings for unfulfilled agreements. The budgets for equipment and library books can be frozen but might generate problems later. For example, when a faculty applicant to a grant is asked whether adequate research equipment is available to conduct specific research, he or she might answer yes in order to receive the grant and strongly urge for more funds to procure the latest equipment.

An even more contentious and costly procedure relating to the library—besides pirating the book budget—can arise from a revenue shortfall so severe that journal subscriptions have to be canceled and refunds obtained. The labor costs and subscription disputes with publishers and subscription jobbers could consume a large share of the refunded subscription money. Expenditure recovery might be a strategy, but it also has its costs; benefits might be realized only in the second or third year after negotiations or court proceedings.

A freeze ordered in the middle of the academic year makes budgetary management very difficult. A freeze on expenditures should be implemented as a temporary measure until the magnitude of the emergency has been determined. A spending freeze reduces managerial flexibility throughout an institution and inevitably centralizes operational authority at the presidential level when the freeze persists for any length of time. Such action reduces the adaptability needed at the point of service delivery to cope effectively with difficult situations and maintain program quality.

Mandated cutbacks. The only event worse than a mid-year academic budget freeze is a mandated budget cutback, which might even include the requirement that funds be returned to the government (usually the state). The need to bear all of the cuts in the last half of the year places a special burden on the budget for the second term or for the summer term, if scheduled. In many public universities, students are required to enroll in one summer term to help spread the operating cost of facilities over a 12-month period. When this is a state requirement, academic departments might schedule courses in the summer that are not taught during the other terms. If they are required courses for majors, reducing the summer budget might unfairly require students to spend an extra term on campus. Similarly, the department that ordered enough supplies in the early fall for the entire academic year should be well stocked; departments with a casual approach to management might run out of supplies in the spring term or early summer.

It should be realized, however, that an early commitment of funds for supplies and travel leaves a department without a pool of funds to relinquish if a mid-season cutback occurs within the budget. It is ironical that a well-managed institution with a reasonable administrative overhead might also feel a real pinch when it is ordered to reduce its administrative costs; such specific demands might be made by state higher education agencies. Only good planning, forecasting, insight, and good luck can lead the department or college administrator to be adequately prepared during economic hard times.

There are times when a double dose of financial difficulty hits an institution or system (Weiss 1990). In the fall of 1990, City University of New York experienced an increased enrollment at the same time its public funding was cut deeply. Although CUNY has had an open admissions policy in its 21 institutions for about 20 years, it now has had to limit admissions at the four-year schools because not enough funds exist to permit the system to hire the teachers needed. As a result, 2,000 classes have been cut from a roster of more than 100,000.

The state's $800 million-plus contribution to the CUNY budget was cut by $29 million; the funds from New York City were down $13 million to about $160 million. Tuition made up the remainder of the $1.1 billion budget; however, government officials have prevented any rise in tuition for two years. Thus, classes are getting larger throughout the CUNY system. The four-year institutions are referring students to the public community colleges, which also are growing rapidly. Even the community colleges need more funds for more classes.

In effect, although perhaps unintended, this referral process is shifting instructional costs from a higher cost sector to one where costs are likely to be lower. Public universities in other states sometimes follow the same procedure when their legislatures or system boards set admissions standards differently for two-year, four-year, and graduate institutions, or when they set enrollment caps for campuses (Mingle 1981). Caps curb enrollment at the more prestigious, largest, and most costly campuses.

Salary and benefit cuts. Perhaps one of the best clues to the nature and duration of a financial emergency is the estimated impact on salaries and benefits in the *next* fiscal year. It is understandable to propose to postpone a salary increase until mid year (December to February) in order to see if the revenues arrive as projected. However, indefinitely postponing salary increases is a decision of great consequence. It can erode morale or create a lifeboat-survival mentality. It reduces or cancels the funds awarded to faculty who are promoted; it prevents, unless otherwise arranged, matching salary offers for faculty being lured by other institutions and it prevents adjustments for pay and other inequities.

A worse situation than postponing salary increases is denying raises entirely. But that's not all. Usually the cost of fringe benefits or income and other taxes continue to rise, so real income for faculty is given a double cut in purchasing power: inflationary reduction and increased benefit costs. Worst of all, of course, would be to affect an actual cut in salary plus these other reductions.

Position reduction. One of the most difficult situations both administrators and faculty must confront is the need to reduce the size of the faculty and staff. This action indicates the severity of the financial difficulty and starts the transition to the long-term strategies needed for institutional survival. At this stage of a financial emergency—often the second year—the funds for unfilled positions would have been sequestered. The next target would be furloughing or terminating nontenured faculty—those people expected to bring new ideas and renewal to an institution.

The budget strategy here is to reduce salary costs. Some of the savings could be used to hire less-expensive part-timers, while another part of the savings might be used for salary raises for the survivors. This strategy often is accompanied by a requirement that the remaining faculty increase their teaching or other work loads. Occasionally, faculty members collectively will decide to take a reduction in pay (perhaps 5 percent) to retain their colleagues and their current work-load patterns. Whether the current mix of faculty is cost effective and worth preserving is the hard question facing administrators.

It should be noted that support staff members might receive job or salary cuts earlier, deeper, and for longer durations. In the spring of 1991, government officials in several states proposed that public employees be requested to voluntarily reduce their work time by 30 to 40 hours without compensation to help balance the 1990-91 budget. Many staff members would rather take such furloughs than lose their jobs; however, job reduction might be unavoidable. The consequence of all of these postponements and cuts is lowered instructional costs—and possibly lowered quality of the educational experience as well. Of course, if enrollments decline or shift out of low-cost majors such as education to higher cost majors in science and technology, then instructional costs might rise.

Position reductions made without systematic program reviews and long-range planning clearly indicate a financial emergency—of whatever duration. One way to prepare for this difficult task is to maintain the results of ongoing program reviews ready to use in a financial emergency.

Confronting long-term financial difficulties
Before the perception is clear that a long-term financial problem is at hand, a number of strategies will be attempted to alleviate the current revenue and cost problems. A multi-year decline or steady figures in enrollment and revenues typically is met with plans to restructure the institution to expand enrollment. The single-sex institution tries to become co-educational; the church-related institution might distance itself from its church sponsor to attract more students and gifts. Programs such as business minors for liberal arts students might be added. Institutions might try to expand vertically by increasing the level of degrees offered: two-year to four-year, four-year to master's, and comprehensive to doctoral and research degrees. Enrollment management becomes necessary to produce enough students to obtain state funding or enough tuition to pay the instructional costs of continuing degree programs.

The 1990s dip in the number of high school graduates has led many private institutions to expend more funds on enrollment marketing as they compete vigorously with one another for applicants; that increases the administrative costs of each institution unless cooperative arrangements are made to control these costs, such as a common application for admission and student aid funds. (Unfortunately, the federal government says that institutional collaboration in some of these matters amounts to collusion.) Similarly, the special and expanded efforts to retain recruited students generates costs but are expected to increase revenues in two or four years and thereafter. When it appears that enrollment and revenues cannot be increased, then it becomes necessary to consider faculty reductions, including even the part-timers; this is the prime cost control strategy in labor-intensive educational institutions.

Terminating programs is one of the most commonly considered long-range financial management strategies. The dean of Yale College is reported to have explained Yale's approach to deficit reduction: "We're hoping to find something that can be expendable rather than try to bleed everybody" (DePalma 1991, p. B8). The reasons for terminating programs are to control quality, use resources efficiently, and then to reduce expenditures; the entire process might take three or more years. Institutions that wish to remain accredited must determine how to adhere to standards while managing to avoid forcing a cutback of programs or program quality.

The reasons for terminating programs are to control quality, use resources efficiently, and then to reduce expenditures.

Public institutions face mandatory cutbacks when a legislature begins reducing its subsidies. Several Oregon state institutions proposed to close down programs: the college of education at Oregon State, teacher education (and 22 other programs) at the University of Oregon, and the school of health and human performance and 12 other programs at Portland State (Monaghan 1991). Even the Oregon community colleges were expected to have to place limits on their admissions; all of the universities were expected to cut enrollments. Given that Oregon voters changed the state and local system of financing government, the state university cuts are expected to be severe and permanent. Reducing programs might be a continuing activity for several years as Oregon's public institutions attempt to balance revenues and costs. Institutions in many other states found during the 1990-92 recession that government officials demanded their institutions cut continuing expenditures such as faculty; the result could be a reduction of revenues back to 1988-89 levels in constant dollars— a terrible situation for all.

A question is whether program terminations will reduce costs. They typically do not in the short run (Mingle 1981). Expenditures are reduced when faculty and support staff are laid off permanently. However, institutions that honor faculty and staff seniority, whether through collective-bargaining agreements or other arrangements, will be pressed to retain tenured personnel because program termination must be accompanied by thorough cost cutting and attempted revenue enhancements before tenured faculty are laid off. So far, institutions have tended to cut unprotected faculty, staff, and administrators before releasing tenured faculty (Mooney 1991). This practice actually might relatively increase the cost of programs by releasing the most junior and less costly faculty and staff members. It also reduces the number of minority and women faculty hired to create a multi-cultural campus.

Institutions with appropriate resources might offer early retirement programs of half-time employment or offer to buy out continuing contracts to reduce the long-term salary and benefit costs. Within multi-campus systems, faculty might receive employment opportunities at other campuses or other options such as shared appointments. In some instances, programs might be suspended and faculty or staff furloughed rather then terminated (Mooney 1991). The assumption in such cases is that the severe financial circumstances are temporary, although they might last for several years.

In some cases (usually at independent private institutions), a college or university might run a deficit for several years before a widespread consensus that conditions must change hits its governing board, chief administrative staff, and faculty. The key phrase that defines the problem is: "This university (or college) cannot be everything to everybody." That phrase indicates that programs need to be reviewed and those that are not central to the mission of the institution must be maintained in a steady state, pared back, consolidated with other programs, or phased out altogether. At these times, program review becomes a strategic planning exercise wherein the forces of support and competition in the environment are considered along with the strengths and weaknesses of the institution. A formal classification of programs for this purpose has been developed by Vandament (1989).

A strategic planning effort has been reported (Harrison 1990) for independent Fairleigh Dickinson University, which is just 50 years old. The institution had been running a deficit for 16 years, enrollment was declining, and state subsidies were being trimmed. A new public four-year college was opened in the same county as the university's largest campus. The dental school had operated at a deficit for 20 years, but with a state subsidy. However, in 1988, leaders in the state of New Jersey said they expected to discontinue the dental school subsidy entirely after 1990. Fairleigh Dickinson closed the dental school in June 1990. However, it still generates costs:

> *The university had to pay severance to staff members, offer placement services to students transferring to other dental schools, and provide patients with many years' worth of records* (p. A33).

The new president reported that the situation could be turned around for the university "if we could reduce operating costs by 3 percent and increase revenue." The board of trustees wanted a balanced budget by 1992-93. Even branch campuses could be closed. The most important question about all of the long-term options is whether the institution will have enough time and skill to devise the long-term solutions necessary. Effective strategic planning could provide a needed early warning.

Summary

An uncertain financial future after the short-term management measures have been undertaken leads to a new round of actions designed to help a troubled institution survive. These include increases in tuition and fees, terminating marginal programs, reducing tenured faculty positions, discontinuing part-time faculty, and instituting deeper budget cuts all across the board. During this time, the focus shifts to a permanent reduction of costs and expenditures, because all of the reserve funds will have been consumed and only small increases (at best) in revenues will be expected.

For a private institution, revenues could continue to decline disastrously; excess land, buildings, and equipment might have to be sold. Unless some financial miracle occurs, such as consolidation with a solvent organization or the state's willingness to take over the institution (Mingle 1981), a college might be headed for bankruptcy. A small private college might be overwhelmed when a public institution opens a branch

---

campus in its territory—and the lower tuition of the publicly subsidized campus attracts students away from the higher priced private college. Only creative adjustments would allow the private college to survive.

Management Systems to Control Costs
The preceding description of management strategies to control costs represents a selection of widely used methods. They tend to be problem-oriented and designed to fix whatever appears to be broken. A few systems maintain broader frameworks which emphasize management planning and foresight, which are the tools needed to anticipate rather than just react to financial problems. Two of these methods will be mentioned here, because their application to small liberal arts colleges has been evaluated and reported (Baldridge and Tierney 1979); this report should be consulted for the details about their evaluation study, which forthrightly lists the caveats about their findings.

The two systems involved are management information systems (MIS) and management by objectives (MBO). The implementation of MIS increases the quality of data about the institution and in its more sophisticated form permits the creation of simulation models. MBO provides the systematic estimation of financial and other consequences from an array of alternatives for solving problems. Baldridge and Tierney concluded that "institutions with successful MIS projects reduced variations in per-student expenditures among departments" (p. 9). They found that expenses in the more costly departments were reduced and student/faculty ratios were equalized. Furthermore, "Institutions with successful advanced MIS projects decreased their per-student expenditures" (p. 9). These results make the study of these systems useful for providing the information and analyses necessary to successfully control costs.

MBO contributes significantly to the planning process of institutions, especially so if coupled with a well-developed MIS. In addition, the two systems provided linkages to the budgeting process at some of the studied institutions. Creating a connection between planning and budgeting is the great need for those who have embraced the more contemporary concept of strategic planning (Baldridge and Tierney 1979; see Vandament 1989).

Like many other management "systems," MIS, MBO, and

various budgeting and planning methods require a confluence of necessity, leader-follower support, and integration with the values and norms of a campus culture.* Much needs to be done to successfully manage costs.

It has been reported by Schmidtlein and others that strong leadership, a political consensus among campus faculty and staff, and other support is needed to move from planning to implementing plans. Although it often is very difficult to do much innovative planning and implementing during relatively good financial times, the effects of economic recession and the threats of financial disaster present a unique and important opportunity for a change in cost management.

A variety of strategies and systems exist to manage costs and expenditures. Baldridge and Tierney endorse the use of some of these systems if existing staff can be carefully trained, new specialists are *not* hired, and consultants are used carefully and economically (p. 13). However, adopting and installing good management strategies and systems are actions that must occur before the financial emergency arrives.

*See *Planning for Higher Education* 1989-90. Vol. 18, no. 2.

COST MANAGEMENT PRACTICES—SUMMARY

This section summarizes the more commonly occurring cost management practices that are prescribed and oftentimes used to confront financial problems. Most of the practices included here have been discussed and analyzed in the previous sections. A prescriptive tone is used here to sharpen the presentation, but no single magic formula exists for controlling costs.

Institutional Direction

A clear institutional mission is required when it comes time to consider the programs that are most important to an institution. Specifying the strengths of all programs and their contribution to the central mission of an institution enables funding priorities to be set and resources to be managed in pursuit of educational quality.

There are many systems for classifying programs (Vandament 1989); in addition to centrality of mission are goals, quality, revenue potential, and costs. Each program should be ranked within the institution. For example, programs can be clustered into four groups: First are the strongest and most valued programs which require a high investment of funds to stay on top and supplements if their instructional income does not equal their costs. Second are the programs of promise that require nurturing and additional funding if they are to begin to move toward achieving their potential; long-term growth and development is required.

A third class of programs are average within an institution, necessary for its mission, but exhibit only a few outstanding elements. Funding is needed to reward those who achieve distinction and to bolster quality. Finally, a fourth group of programs appear to be tangential to the main purposes of an institution and provide few connections to or support of other programs. This group must be reviewed regularly to determine if its resources could be used advantageously in other programs or for new programs. Level funding or reduced funding might be in order. From this group must come the funds for institutional adaptation and growth.

A clear mission statement and programmatic priorities are a necessary but not sufficient condition to ensure that costs are understood and controlled. Data about costs need to be collected, analyzed, and interpreted. Policy criteria about work loads, minimum-size classes, and other factors are required so that management judgments can be made about the most productive, efficient, and effective use of resources. These

needs have been around for more than 60 years; one wonders why they haven't successfully been implemented.

The great fear about using this grand strategy to manage costs is that it seems destined to grind up loyal faculty and staff in the maw of efficiency. Furthermore, to many organizational analysts, the strategy appears to be a linear model of administration (and governance) in which exists no conflicting goals, no active interest groups articulating and pursuing different value positions, and no outside patrons and constituencies with very particular views about higher education. However, many people recognize the need to bring some order to the blooming, buzzing organized anarchy that Cohen and March (1974) described, especially when financial difficulties arise. Some authorities are skeptical that a new "order" is possible given the factors identified by Cohen and March.

Whether colleges and universities can ever perform the planning and analysis that will allow them to accurately anticipate the future and thrive on it—even when financial problems arise—is an open question (see *Change* 1990). For those who want to try, the tools and techniques are available; one of the newest systems designed to enhance planning is total quality management (Coate 1990).

Anticipating the Future

College and university revenues are affected directly by changes in the federal, state, and local economies. Government response to the state of the economy translates into shifts in revenues for higher education. The availability of student aid funds, amounts of tuition needed, and residential living costs all respond to economic conditions and government action.

Demographic changes such as births and migration increase or decrease the number of high school graduates and their propensity to enroll, stimulate changes in enrollment levels. Institutional proximity to students and availability of professional and occupational courses stimulate adult enrollment. The availability of several postsecondary institutions with different price structures affects enrollment, revenues, and costs. A recession often stimulates people to return to college to upgrade their skills, complete degree programs, or prepare for new careers.

Each institution needs some way to forecast the external

events most likely to affect its well-being. Strategic planning, futures research, cross-impact studies, environmental scanning, and any other reliable procedures can be used by planners, institutional or policy researchers, or administrators to note the trends affecting the resources and costs of their institutions. Both short- and long-range policy emphases and data trends are important, especially in forecasting revenues and costs. The purpose of accurately forecasting revenues and costs should not be forgotten: to enable institutional administrators to maximize revenues and to minimize costs until a dynamic balance of resources allows production of services at an acceptable level of cost and quality. This purpose must be used by top leaders as one of the criteria in periodically evaluating the success of all institutional administrators.

Administrative Compliance

The old concept of accountability is emerging again as Congress and state legislatures request documentation about the need for resources and an explanation of how the resources are used. The 30 percent ceiling on loan default rates, the sharpening of definitions about what may be included in calculating grant overhead reimbursement rates, and many other stipulations are requiring compliance before revenues are received, renewed, or retained. Many states are requiring more elaborate statements of need for new programmatic (incentive) funding; in some instances, this will be the only way to receive new funds.

The 1991 Florida Legislature changed to a partial lump-sum funding appropriation for the State University System in exchange for its agreement to develop a detailed accountability reporting system using indicators about all manner of university inputs, processes, and outputs. Is this déjà vu?

To maximize revenues, both administrative compliance and accountability reporting increasingly are being demanded. Institutions might have to increase their administrative costs to develop the capability to fully and accurately report the data and information needed. Institutional research might have to be reinvented or expanded to again focus on costs.

The connection between cost increases and tuition levels are being widely scrutinized. Again, institutional justifications should be documented clearly with accurate and complete data. When tuition levels are raised to provide continuation funding as in many states with reduced appropriations, that

is important information.

When tuitions need to be increased to obtain funding for new programs, the documentation should be crystal clear. The next question to be expected from the funders being asked for new dollars is: "Why don't you drop a low-priority program to obtain part of these needed funds?" Legislative staff are saying quietly, "Show us the results of your good-faith efforts to cut duplicate and unattractive programs and to enhance undergraduate teaching, so we can believe that you do have a genuine financial need." In these circumstances, an institution has to decide how far it will allow itself to be co-opted by the legislature's goals and priorities in order to obtain new dollars. When questions like these are received, they can be used as the basis for a serious program review.

Program Changes for Revenues
Presuming Bowen's previously cited principles are correct, the needs of higher education are infinite and thus all available revenues will be spent to satisfy some portion of existing needs, with demands left over. Although needs are infinite, resources are finite; this truism confronts us repeatedly during difficult financial times. The ongoing task is to balance revenues and expenditures.

When the cost-income crunch comes, one element of a coping strategy is to take any reasonable-seeming action in order to increase revenues. If declining enrollments cause reduced revenues, then programs need to be reviewed for their attractiveness (for example, a business minor for liberal arts students), new student markets sought, and all sources of income squeezed for more revenues (this might include raising tuition). Enrollment-management policies may be established to encourage nontraditional and adult students and special services developed for the large population of commuting students (Jacoby 1989).

Institutions also find that they sometimes must raise more revenues to spend on services that will attract and hold a particular income group of students. We now see evidence that potential students are impressed by the way a campus looks; they also link their vision of a quality education with its tuition price. A recent study indicates they might have some grounds for that belief, although the relationship is not a certainty (Gilmore 1990).

One of the many difficult financial crunches to deal with

is that generated by mandated expenditures—for example, social security, health insurance, and other legislated programs of social policy. Apart from the merits of these programs is the fact that revenues aren't received to cover even part of their costs. These mandated expenditures need to be captured in the overhead expenses the institution must "charge" all of its programs. Thus, to obtain true costs for a college program, one needs to include a dollar amount that incorporates the cost of institutional direction and leadership, libraries, central services such as purchasing, utilities, and so on. Similarly, true costs of a program include the cost of equipment and facilities and the funds necessary to install, begin, and keep everything running.

One of the many difficult financial crunches to deal with is that generated by mandated expenditures.

Responding to Cost Pressures

Current costs, their history, and their likely direction must be known in order to manage them. In addition, emerging new or different costs must be identified and their likely demand on current and future revenues estimated. Mandated programs and other unavoidable costs require special attention, as mentioned previously. These should be scheduled to be reassessed at least annually (semiannually, if possible) to keep up with the trends.

When cost increases appear likely, the revenues to pay for them must be estimated; then, if the amounts appear to be too great, alternative goods or services should be sought. Expanding instructional work loads for faculty also need to be considered. Unfortunately, many colleges seem unable to identify such alternatives; this inability needs to be studied and comparable institutions and national organizations like NACUBO should be inquired of. Payments to local taxing districts, hospitals, and other local service providers in lieu of paying local taxes is an important example of a nearly inescapable cost.

Administrative costs are a growing concern of funders and legislators. A full description from a large sample of colleges and universities of these costs—including the reasons why their requirements change over time and other relevant explanations—are badly needed. Interinstitutional comparisons are important.

Most administrators sense that mandated social programs and requirements from state legislatures and higher education system agencies are responsible for a portion of the added administrative expenses. Administrative computing also is seen as a factor here. More counseling and advising services for students is another possible source of increasing expenses. These and the addition of all types of technical support staff deserve careful scrutiny, for they have taken at least two percentage points of aggregate expenditures over the past decade.

Faculty and Staff Salary Issues

Salary costs need to be studied on several grounds: Are they competitive for the quality of institution? Are they continuing to lose ground to inflation, declining institutional revenues, and salaries at other comparable institutions? Do they serve to motivate high-quality performance? Does salary compression and inversion exist, and have these elements created a morale problem? Are salaries fair by rank, experience, race, gender, and discipline? Are there enough or too many part-time, temporary faculty? Are the salaries of part-timers "fair"? College and faculty deans and other academic officers, assisted by institutional researchers, should regularly and systematically analyze salaries.

Fringe-benefit programs represent cost areas in which some components are increasing rapidly with limited available alternatives. Social security and health insurance are two of the most expensive areas. Self-insurance for a consortia of colleges might be a way to control insurance costs. Retirement programs also are important, for they tend to be the largest single fringe-benefit item. Retirement payments also are significant, because they might hold the key to a reduction of high instructional costs from an aging and expensive faculty. The need to have cost-of-living escalator clauses in these programs is an important retirement incentive but could be expensive during inflationary times.

Little consensus exists regarding the rate at which faculty members are expected to retire. The state of the economy and the elimination in 1994 of the 70-year-old employment cap might stimulate faculty to retire later than age 65. Other fringe-benefit programs (such as faculty housing) can push up costs, but little is known about these.

Another important faculty cost issue stems from the average work load, which usually is considered in terms of instructional classroom or credit hours. There is spotty evidence that the number of courses being taught has declined over the past 20 years; others say faculty now are teaching one month less than they were about 20 years ago. Uniform and comparable data are needed to document the average work load of faculty; no such data currently exists. However, self-reported work-load data indicates that faculty in larger institutions and research universities spend more time at their jobs than other faculty, although two-year faculty say they teach more students even if they work fewer hours.

There is a slight indication that several states again are reviewing the need for laws to precisely declare the number of hours public-institution faculty members should teach. Every institution needs to know the average teaching load of faculty as well as the criteria for equalizing this load and any other data that correctly illustrate the direct cost of instruction. The obvious question that needs answering is whether a decline in faculty work load has occurred and whether this decline has driven up instructional costs.

Other Instructional Costs

Using audio and video materials, electronic systems, more traditional learning facilities such as laboratories and libraries, and computer applications of all kinds potentially could push up instructional costs. The electronic systems have not yet supplanted regular faculty instructors, but they do add to the typical costs of instruction. Some costs such as scholarly and scientific journals have increased in price by as much as 25 percent a year.

If state revenues flatten out—as they are in many states— or decline for a few years, distance learning with simultaneous teaching at different sites using satellite technology might be tried as a substitute for full-time faculty at distant locations. These experiments are expensive, but might be useful in times of short revenues. If the decision to use these electronic systems is made primarily because of the relative low cost of operation, then the quality of learning needs to be verified. Faculty members aren't the only people who might have second thoughts about these systems. Most students and parents also have very traditional expectations about the nature of classroom instruction—the desirability of a real, live, genuine professor in the classroom, for example.

Research Expenses

Although not a typical cost at most colleges and universities, research expenses and revenues are important components of the budgets of most large institutions, including comprehensive and doctoral research universities. At the same time that the cost of research equipment and facilities continue to rise, the federal government continues to reduce its share of funding for basic research even when its research funding is increasing.

Very grave differences of opinion exist regarding what constitutes the true cost of research at universities. The federal government, which is the largest funder, is redefining what it believes are true research costs. These specifications will be crucial information to all universities that need to recover the full costs of research. Many universities will have to generate a new study of overhead rate charges if Congress is successful in limiting overhead to 25 percent

The support staff devoted to research (who comprise about 75 percent of those engaged in this function—faculty is the other 25 percent) have been one of the fastest growing segments of higher education. The supporting staff deserves careful study for duplication, need for full-time practitioners, and other characteristics such as shared use, and such. Committees of non-scientists and scientists periodically should review the use of research support staff; this can be accomplished during the periodic program reviews.

Managing and Controlling Costs
One should examine every inch of a gift horse. The consequences of accepting a gift without having the funds to fully utilize or operate the service or facility related to it can generate costs for many years. Legislative "gifts" of buildings, equipment, and special programs that haven't been on an institution's wish list could have similar drawbacks. Operational costs for these beneficences need to be estimated and and explained to government officials.

A focus by an institution on raising revenues through increased enrollment requires market analysis and probably more administrative costs. It also requires estimates of secondary consequences such as the costs for additional services to the students and the need for more instructors. Estimating the unexpected consequences of all revenues and cost-saving proposals is important to ensure that later costs will not make a current financial problem worse in future years. Even cost-conservation programs need periodic review to ensure they generate savings after the first major effort of implementation.

It should be clear that in a labor-intensive organization like a college or university, a time will come when the only strategy for controlling costs is to reduce the salary budget. Saving funds through attrition—that is, choosing not to fill new vacant positions or those resulting from employees exiting— is a common approach. However, an indiscriminate freezing of all vacant positions, like an across-the-board budget cut, can be harmful to high-priority programs.

In order to manage costs purposefully, a clear mission and set of program priorities must be established, as discussed previously. Every three to five years, each program (educational, administrative, student service, etc.) should be reviewed. The review should focus on the quality of a program and whether its revenues and costs are balanced and its priority classification should change; also, some timetable should be provided to improve or reduce staffing. In this way, revenue requests or cost reductions can focus on specific programs or their important aspects. If it's necessary to change the program mix in an institution, to send staff or faculty on furlough, or to reduce employees—especially tenured faculty—then these program review reports clearly should support such decisions.

One way to stave off the very unpleasant task and the effects of cutting employees is to continuously monitor the use of resources, noting which programs have quality and revenue problems, and make adjustments as needed. In other words, don't wait until a financial crunch of costs and revenues arrives. It should be noted that many administrators believe they have inadequate authority or legitimacy to make staffing reductions. They like to wait for a financial emergency of some kind before acting, using the emergency as the grounds for an unpalatable decision. Establishing public criteria for making decisions about programs would be helpful.

Any number of indicators are useful in diagnosing the financial health of an institution. These indicators need to become explicit and codified; reports should be generated monthly or quarterly to members of the institution's central administration to stimulate program reviews and corrective action. When the short-term financial emergency arrives, a freeze on purchasing, travel, and vacancy fulfillment usually occurs first. The focus is to reduce expenditures but save existing services and filled positions. The latter might require transferring funds from reserve accounts to continue all activities—especially those activities that generate revenues. Part-time faculty might be added to save salary costs, and some of the vacant positions might be cut permanently. Specialty classes might be cut along with their part-time faculty if such individuals were hired exclusively to teach these classes. Salary increases might be reduced or not offered at all.

In the longer term financial crisis, equity issues and prudent management might be set aside. The need for employee furloughs or terminations should depend upon program reviews and strategic planning assessments. Under these conditions, cuts are made initially among part-time faculty who teach required courses; later, cuts might be made in some tenured positions. These actions all occur to reduce the salary and fringe-benefit costs. Where possible, faculty and staff may elect to take salary cuts to save jobs. This action must be carefully evaluated to determine if all programs should be saved or only those rated central to the mission of the institution. A continued decline in revenues leads to sale of surplus land and buildings and likely use of some endowment assets. Even with all of these actions, survival is not guaranteed.

The preceding strategies and tactics to reduce costs during financial emergencies have all the defects of ad hoc actions. But this need not be the case. Various planning and management systems can be built to formally and systematically monitor use of institutional resources and clearly identify the actions needed to build a viable financial future. The appropriate strategy is to mobilize all the people who have a stake in the future of an institution, and then base cost control plans on accurate data and information.

REFERENCES

The Educational Resources Information Center (ERIC) Clearinghouse on Higher Education abstracts and indexes the current literature on higher education for inclusion in ERIC's data base and announcement in ERIC's monthly bibliographic journal, *Resources in Education* (RIE). Most of these publications are available through the ERIC Document Reproduction Service (EDRS). For publications cited in this bibliography that are available from EDRS, ordering number and price code are included. Readers who wish to order a publication should write to the ERIC Document Reproduction Service, 7420 Fullerton Rd., Suite 110, Springfield, VA 22153-2852. (Phone orders with VISA or MasterCard are taken at 800-443-ERIC or 703-440-1400.) When ordering, please specify the document (ED) number. Documents are available as noted in microfiche (MF) and paper copy (PC). If you have the price code ready when you call EDRS, an exact price can be quoted. The last page of the latest issue of *Resources in Education* also has the current cost, listed by code.

"Academic Strategy: Five Years Later." February 1988. *AAHE Bulletin.* An interview with George Keller.

Allen, R., and P. Brinkman. 1983. *Marginal Costing Techniques.* Boulder, Colo.: National Center for Higher Education Management Systems (NCHEMS). ED 246 816. 85 pp. MF–01; PC–04.

Allen, R., and E.E. Chaffee. 1981. *Management Fads in Higher Education.* Monograph #3. Boulder, Colo.: NCHEMS. ED 205 098. 35 pp. MF–01; PC–02.

Amberg, J. 1989. "Higher (-Priced) Education." *American Scholar* 58: 521-32. EJ396779.

Anderson, R.E., and J.W. Meyerson. 1990. *Financing Higher Education in a Global Economy.* New York: Macmillan.

Andrew, L.D., and R. Russo. October 1989. "Who Gets What?: Impact of Financial Aid Policies." *Research in Higher Education* 30: 471-83.

"Annual Report on the Economic Status of the Profession." March-April 1991. *Academe.*

Astin, A.W. 1982. *Minorities in American Higher Education.* San Francisco: Jossey-Bass.

Astin, A.W., and C.J. Inouye. 1988. "How Public Policy at the State Level Affects Private Higher Education Institutions." *Economics of Education Review* 7: 47-63.

Balderston, F.E. 1974. *Managing Today's University.* San Francisco: Jossey-Bass.

———. 1990. "Organization, Funding, Incentives, and Initiatives for University Research: A University Management Perspective." In *The Economics of American Universities,* edited by S.A. Hoenack and E.L. Collins. Albany, N.Y.: State University of New York Press.

Baldridge, J.V., and M.L. Tierney. 1979. *New Approaches to Management.* San Francisco: Jossey-Bass.

Baltes, P.C. 1987-88. "Fiscal Stress and Implications for Planning." *Planning for Higher Education* 16(4): 3-18.

Bender, L.W. 1989. "Fund Raising to Assure College Library Vitality." *Community College Review* 17(1): 1+.

Bennett, W. November 26, 1986. Text of Secretary Bennett's speech on college costs and U.S. student aid. *Chronicle of Higher Education* 33: A20-22.

Berdahl, R.O., and S.M. Studds. 1989. "The Tension of Excellence and Equity: The Florida Enhancement Programs." College Park, Md.: National Center for Postsecondary Governance and Finance, University of Maryland.

Bernstein, A. 1989. "Ivy at a Bargain?" *Change* 21(2): 4.

Blumenstyk, G., and C. Myers. August 16, 1989. "For Most, Cost of Going to College Outpaces Inflation Again: U.S. Probes Tuition and Student Aid on 20 Private Campuses." *Chronicle of Higher Education*: A1+.

Bowen, H.R. 1980. *The Costs of Higher Education*. San Francisco: Jossey-Bass.

―――. 1981. "Cost Differences: The Amazing Disparity Among Institutions of Higher Education in Educational Costs Per Student." *Change* 13(1): 21-27.

Bowen, H., and G. Douglas. 1973. *Efficiency in Liberal Education*. Berkeley, Ca.: Carnegie Commission on Higher Education.

Bowen, W.G., and J.A. Sousa. 1989. *Prospects for Faculty in the Arts and Sciences*. Lawrenceville, N.J.: Princeton University Press.

Breckon, D.J. January 4, 1989. "On the Roller-Coaster Ride of a College Presidency, a Sense of Humor is Essential." *Chronicle of Higher Education*: B2-3.

Breneman, D.W. January/February 1990. "Time for Honesty." *Change*: 9.

Brinkman, P. 1988. *The Cost of Providing Higher Education: A Conceptual Overview*. Denver: State Higher Education Executive Officers. ED 299 877. 34 pp. MF–01; PC–02.

Brown, M.K. 1989. "Developing and Implementing a Process for the Review of Nonacademic Units." *Research in Higher Education*: 30+.

Business Officer. May 1991. Monthly publication of NACUBO.

Carnegie Commission on Higher Education. 1972. *More Effective Use of Resources*. New York: McGraw-Hill.

Chaney, B., and E. Farris. 1990. *The Finances of Higher Education Institutions*. Washington, D.C.: Office of Planning, Budget and Evaluation, U.S. Department of Education. ED 327 110. 82 pp. MF–01; PC–04.

Change. November/December 1990. Various articles on cost management.

Chaudhari, P. 1985. Statement in *The University Research Infrastructure* 1986: 270-94.

Cheit, E.F. 1971. *The New Depression in Higher Education*. New York: McGraw-Hill.

————. 1973. *The New Depression in Higher Education—Two Years Later*. New York: The Carnegie Foundation for the Advancement of Teaching.

Cheney, L.V. 1990. *Tyrannical Machines: A Report on Educational Practices Gone Wrong and Our Best Hopes for Setting Them Right*. Washington, D.C.: National Endowment for the Humanities.

Coate, L.E. 1990. "TQM on Campus: Implementing Total Quality Management in a University Setting." *Business Officer* 4(5): 26-35.

Cohen, M.D., and J.G. March. 1974. *Leadership and Ambiguity*. New York: McGraw-Hill.

Collison, N-K. June 7, 1989. "Officials Warn of a Crisis in Student Health Insurance as Medical Costs Soar and Companies Revise Policies." *Chronicle of Higher Education*: A31-2.

Cope, R.G. 1987. *Opportunity from Strength: Strategic Planning Clarified with Case Examples*. ASHE-ERIC Higher Education Reports No. 87-8. Washington, D.C.: ERIC Clearinghouse on Higher Education. ED 296 694. 149 pp. MF–01; PC–06.

DePalma, A. January 30, 1991. "Yale Plans Cuts as Income Falls and Costs Rise." *New York Times*: B8.

Eisner, L., ed. 1988. *A Call for Clarity: Income, Loans, Cost, Issues*. Washington, D.C.: American Association of State Colleges and Universities. ED 293 397. 52 pp. MF–01; PC–03.

El-Khawas, E. 1987. *Campus Trends*. Washington, D.C.: American Council on Education. ED 286 402. 52 pp. MF–01; PC–03.

Fairweather, J.S., R.M. Hendrickson, and S.H. Russell. 1990. "A Portrait of the Full-Time Faculty Position: Activities and Workload." Revised draft of special issue report no. 2. Washington, D.C.: National Center for Education Statistics.

Federal Support for Education: Fiscal Years 1980-1990. May 1991. National Center for Education Statistics 96-631. Washington, D.C.: U.S. Department on Education.

Financing Managing University Research Equipment. 1985. In *University Research Infrastructure*. 1986. Appendix 3.

Fischer, F.J. 1990. "State Financing of Higher Education: A New Look at an Old Problem." *Change* 22(1): 42-56.

"Flashcard." November 4, 1990. *New York Times*. EDUC: 12.

Frances, C. 1990. *What Factors Affect College Tuition? A Guide to the Facts and Issues*. Washington, D.C.: American Association of State Colleges and Universities. E 317 149. 71 pp. MF–01; PC–03.

Franck, G., R. Anderson, and C. Bernard. 1987. "Tax Reform and Higher Education." New Directions for Higher Education No. 58: 9–19.

Freeman, R. 1976. *The Overeducated American*. New York: Academic Press.

Fuchsberg, G. July 27, 1988. "$20 Billion Needed to Save Crumbling

Campus Buildings, a Survey Finds." *Chronicle of Higher Education*: A13.

————. January 4, 1989. "Johns Hopkins U. to Cut Arts-and- Sciences Faculty by 10 Pct. and Take Other Steps to Stem Deficits in Several Divisions." *Chronicle of Higher Education*: A31-32.

Galambos, E.C. 1988. "Higher Education Administrative Costs and Staffing." In *Higher Education Administrative Costs: Continuing the Study.* T.P. Snyder and E.C. Galambos. 1988.

Gilmartin, K.J. 1984. "Measuring the Viability of Colleges." *American Educational Research Journal* 21: 79-101.

Gilmore, J.L. 1990. *Price and Quality in Higher Education.* Washington, D.C.: Office of Educational Research and Improvement, U.S. Department of Education. ED 326 146. 147 pp. MF–01; PC–06.

Ginsberg, S.G. 1982. "120 Ways to Increase Income and Decrease Expenses." *Business Officer* 16: 14-16.

Gladieux, L.E. May/June 1985. "The Student Loan Quandary: Are There Workable Alternatives?" *Change* 21: 35-41.

Gold, L.N. 1990. *Tuition Formulas at Work: An Examination of States that Use a Numerical Formula to Help Set Public College Tuition.* Washington, D.C.: American Association of State Colleges and Universities.

Gold, S.D. 1989-90. "State Support of Higher Education: A National Perspective." *Journal of College and University Planning* 18: 21-33.

Grassmuck, K. March 28, 1990. "Big Increases in Academic-Support Staffs Prompt Growing Concerns on Campuses." *Chonicle of Higher Education*: A1.

Greenberg, M.W. 1988. "What's Happened to College Tuitions and Why: A View from a Public University." *The College Board Review* 147: 13-15+.

Hamlin, A., and C. Hungerford. May/June 1989. "How Private Colleges Survive Financial Crisis." *AGB Reports* 31: 17-22.

Hansen, J.S. 1988. "Pay Now, Go Later." *College Board Review* 147: 8-11+.

Harrison, C. October 31, 1990. "With Falling Enrollment and a $24 Million Deficit, Fairleigh Dickinson U. Prepares for Retrenchment." *Chronicle of Higher Education*: A31-33.

Hartle, T. Spring/Summer 1986. "Beneath the Surface: College Is Not as Costly as It Seems." *Educational Record* 67: 16-19.

————. January/February 1990. "Federal Support for Higher Education in the '90s: Boom, Bust, or Something in Between." *Change*: 32-41.

Hauptman, A. 1990. *The College Tuition Spiral.* Washington, D.C.: American Council on Education.

————. 1990. *The College Tuition Spiral.* A Report to the College Board and the American Council on Education. New York: Macmillan.

————. March 6, 1991. "Financial Incentives, Not Regulation, Are Needed to Reform the Student-Aid Process." *Chronicle of Higher Education*: B2-3.

Henderson, C. 1988. "Looking Ahead at Student Expenses." *Adademe* 74(5): 32-35.

Hensley, O.D. 1985. Statement on research support personnel. In *University Research Infrastructure*.

Hexter, H. 1990. "Faculty Salaries in Perspective." *Research Briefs* [ACE] 1: 1-7.

Higher Education Costs. 1988. Hearing before the Subcommittee on Postsecondary Education of the Committee on Education and Labor, U.S. House of Representatives, 1987. No. 100-47. Washington, D.C.: U.S. Government Printing Office.

Hines, E.R. 1989. "State Support of Higher Education from Expansion to Steady State or Decline, 1969 to 1989, Including an Illinois Case Study." Normal, Ill.: Center for the Study of Educational Finance. ED 309 700. 31 pp. MF–01; PC–02.

Hoenack, S.A., and E.L. Collins, eds. 1990. *The Economics of American Universities*. Albany, N.Y.: State University of New York Press.

Horwitz, M.D., and R.L. Rolett. January 1991. "Retirement Communities: A Financially Rewarding Educational Approach." *Business Officer* 24: 33-35.

Hug, J. 1989. "Research Facilities Needs Soar." *Education Record* 70(1): 29-32.

Hyatt, J.A. 1988-89. "Financing Facilities Renewal and Replacement." *Planning For Higher Education* 17(3): 33-42.

Hyatt, J.A., and A.A. Santiago. 1986. *Financial Management of Colleges and Universities*. Washington, D.C.: NACUBO.

Jacoby, B. 1989. *The Student as Commuter: Developing a Comprehensive Institutional Response*. ASHE-ERIC Higher Education Report No. 89-7. Washington, D.C.: ERIC Clearinghouse on Higher Education. ED 319 298. 118 pp. MF–01; PC–05.

Jaschik, S. January 11, 1989. "Iowa's Recovering Economy Brings New Scrutiny, Not New Money, Colleges Find." *Chronicle of Higher Education*: A1+.

Jellema, W.W. 1973. *From Red to Black?* San Francisco: Jossey-Bass.

Jenkins, R. February 1991. "Growth Slows: Average Endowment's Return Was 9.6 Percent in 1990." *Business Officer*: 18-23.

————. "Budget Blues for the Nation's Colleges and Universities." *Academe* 74: 12-16.

Jensen, E.L. 1981. "Student Financial Aid and Persistence in College." *Journal of Higher Education* 52(3): 280-94.

————. 1984. "Student Financial Aid and Degree Attainment." *Research in Higher Education* 20(1): 117-27.

Jewett, F.I. August 16, 1989. Letter to editor on faculty shortages. *Chronicle of Higher Education*: B4.

Johnstone, D.B. November/December 1990. "Productivity and Cost

Containment: An Apologia, or 'So What Else Is New?'" *Change*: 54-55.

Kaiser, H. 1989. "Rebuilding the Campus." *Educational Record* 70: 4-7+.

Karelis, C.H., and R.D. Sabot. 1987. "Financing Higher Education." *Liberal Education* 73: 40-42.

Keller, G. 1983. *Academic Strategy: The Management Revolution in American Higher Education*. Baltimore: Johns Hopkins University Press.

Kirshstein, R.J., and D.R. Sherman, V.K. Tikoff, C. Masten, and J. Fairweather. 1990. *The Escalating Costs of Higher Education*. Washington, D.C.: Office of Planning, Budget, and Evaluation, U.S. Department of Education. ED 328 114. 161 pp. MF– 01; PC–07.

Kleiman, C. January 2, 1991. "College Lures Parental-Minded Professors With Paid-Leave Policy." *Tallahassee Democrat*: 3D.

Koch, J.V. October 1982. "Salary Equity Issues in Higher Education: Where Do We Stand? *AAHE Bulletin*: 7-14. ED 222 162. 9 pp. MF– 01; PC–01.

Kolodny, A. February 6, 1991. "Colleges Must Recognize Students' Cognitive Styles and Cultural Backgrounds." *Chronicle of Higher Education*: A44.

Kramon, G. March 24, 1991. "Medical Insurers Vary Fees to Aid Healthier People." *New York Times*: 1+.

"The Lattice and the Ratchet." June 1990. *Policy Perspectives* 2: 1-8 [Pew Higher Education Research Program].

Leslie, D.L. May 10, 1991. Personal communication.

Leslie, L.L., and P.T. Brinkman. 1988. *The Economic Value of Higher Education*. New York: Macmillan Publishing Co.

Martin, D. May 1988. "Understanding the Costs of College." *Phi Delta Kappan*: 673-76.

McDuff, N.G. 1990. "Financing the Costs of Higher Education: Planning Creative Student and Institutional Options." *Planning for Higher Education* 18: 15-33.

McMillen, L. August 16, 1989. "Escalating Costs Force Private Research Universities to Scale Back Academic, Administrative Operations." *Chronicle of Higher Education*: A21-22.

———. February 6, 1991. "To Boost Quality and Cut Costs, Oregon State U. Adopts a Customer-Oriented Approach to Campus Services." *Chronicle of Higher Education*: A27-8.

McPherson, M.S., M.O. Schapiro, and G.C. Winston. 1988. "Recent Trends in U.S. Higher Education Costs and Prices: The Role of Government Funding." *American Economic Review* 79: 253-57.

Massy, W.F. 1987. "Making It All Work: Sound Financial Management." *New Directions for Higher Education* 58: 87-102.

Maynard, J. 1971. *Some Microeconomics of Higher Education*. Lincoln: Univ. of Nebraska Press.

Meeth, L.R. 1974. *Quality Education for Less Money*. San Francisco:

Jossey-Bass.

Meisinger, R.J., Jr., and L.W. Dubeck. 1984. *College and University Budgeting.* Washington, D.C.: NACUBO.

Micek, S., ed. 1980. *Integrating Academic Planning and Budgeting in a Rapidly Changing Environment: Process and Technical Issues.* Boulder, Colo: NCHEMS.

Mingle, J.R., and Associates. 1981. *Challenges of Retrenchment.* San Francisco: Jossey-Bass.

Monaghan, P. February 20, 1991. "Oregon Colleges Plan 'Devastating' Surgery to Survive State Cut." *Chronicle of Higher Education:* A25+.

Mooney, C.J. February 27, 1991. "Financial Stresses Hit Professors, but Most Colleges Protect Tenured Ranks." *Chronicle of Higher Education:* A1+.

Morrison, J.L., W.L. Renfro, and W.I. Boucher. 1984. *Futures Research and the Strategic Planning Process.* ASHE-ERIC Higher Education Reports, No. 84-9. Washington, D.C.: ERIC Clearinghouse on Higher Education. ED 259 692. 141 pp. MF–01; PC–06.

Mullen, J.M. 1988. "College Costs and the State Role in Higher Education Funding." *Educational Record* 69: 9-14.

———. 1989. "College Costs." *Educational Record* 69: 9-14.

National Center for Education Statistics. 1990. *Faculty in Higher Education Institutions, 1988.* NCES 90-365. Washington, D.C.: U.S. Government Printing Office. ED 321 628. 209 pp. MF–01; PC–09.

O'Keefe, M. May/June 1986. "College Costs, Have They Gone Too High Too Fast?" *Change:* 4-12.

———. 1987. "Where Does the Money Really Go?" *Change* 19(6): 12-34.

"Opinion Leaders See Rising College Costs as Major Concern." February 24, 1988. *Chronicle of Higher Education:* A36-37.

Pickens, W.H. 1987. *The Infrastructure Needs of California Public Higher Education Through the Year 2000.* Sacramento: California State Postsecondary Education Commission. ED 291 301. 15 pp. MF–01; PC–01.

Policy Perspectives. The Pew Higher Education Research Program. Philadelphia: Univ. of Penn.

Report of the ARL Serials Prices Project. 1989. Washington, D.C.: Association of Research Libraries. ED 311 922. 119 pp. MF–01; PC–05.

Revolution in Higher Education. Baltimore: Johns Hopkins University Press.

Rosenzweig, R.M. February 28, 1990. "Challenges to Test the Mettle of Academe's Best Leaders." *Chronicle of Higher Education:* A44.

Rourke, F.E., and G.E. Brooks. 1966. *The Managerial Revolution in Higher Education.* Baltimore: Johns Hopkins University Press.

Roush, C. March 24, 1991. "Small Employers Ill Over Health Benefits." *Tampa Tribune:* B1+.

Russell, J.D. 1931. *Efficiency in College Management.* Bloomington: Bureau of Cooperative Research, Indiana University.

————. 1954. *The Finance of Higher Education*. Rev. ed. Chicago: University of Chicago Press.

Samuelson, S. March/April 1991. "Mid-Year Revisions: A Summary of a *Grapevine* Survey." *Grapevine*: 3042-3.

Saunders, C.B., Jr. April 3, 1991. "The Broadest Changes in Student Aid in 25 Years Could Be Part of Education Amendments of 1992." *Chronicle of Higher Education*: B1-2.

Schaw, W.A. 1989. "The Time Bomb Continues to Tick." *Educational Record*: 9-11.

"Senior Appointments with Reduced Loads." July/August 1987. *Academe*: 50.

Schmidtlein, F.A. 1989-90. "Why Linking Budgets to Plans Has Proved Difficult in Higher Education." *Planning for Higher Education* 18(2): 9-23.

Schmidtlein, F.A., and T.H. Milton. 1988-89. "College and University Planning: Perspectives from a Nationwide Study." *Planning for Higher Education* 17(3): 1-19.

Sessions, R., and T. Collins. 1988. "More Accountability in Federally Funded Academic Research: A Costly 'Bill of Goods.'" *Journal of the Society of Research Administrators* 20: 195-210.

Snyder, T.P., and E. Galambos. 1988. *Higher Education Administrative Costs: Continuing the Study*. Washington, D.C.: Office of Educational Research and Improvement, U.S. Department of Education. ED 286 460. 90 pp. MF–01; PC–04.

Stampen, J.O., and R.H. Fenske. 1988. "The Impact of Financial Aid on Ethnic Minorities." *Review of Higher Education* 11(4): 337-53.

"State Notes." February 6, 1991. *Chronicle of Higher Education*: A21.

Stevens, E.B., and E.C. Elliott. 1925. *Unit Costs of Higher Education*. New York: Macmillan.

Suttle, J. 1983. "The Rising Costs of Private Higher Education." *Research in Higher Education* 18: 253-70.

Sykes, C.J. 1988. *ProfScam: Professors and the Demise of Higher Education*. Milwaukee, Wis.: Reardon & Walsh.

TIAA-CREF. 1990. *College and University Employee Retirement and Insurance Benefits Cost Survey*. New York: Teachers Insurance and Annuity Association.

Tolbert, P. March 1985. "Institutional Environments and Resource Dependence: Sources of Administrative Structure in Institutions of Higher Education." *Administrative Science Quarterly*: 1-13.

Tough Choices: A Guide to Administrative Cost Management in Colleges and Universities. 1990. Washington, D.C.: Office of Planning, Budget and Evaluation, U.S. Department of Education. ED 327 111. 53 pp. MF–01; PC–03.

Troxler, H. March 26, 1991. "Gorilla's Claws May Be Cut By Lawmakers." *Tampa Tribune*: F1.

Tucker, A. 1986. *Chairing the Academic Department: Leadership*

Among Peers. 2d ed. New York: Macmillan.

Uchitelle, L. June 18, 1990. "Surplus of College Graduates Dims Job Outlook for Others." *New York Times*. A1+.

The University Research Infrastructure and the Federal Government. 1986. Hearings before the Task Force on Science Policy of the Committee on Science and Technology, House of Representatives. 99th Congress, Vol. 6, No. 101. Washington, D.C.: U.S. Government Printing Office.

Vandament, W.E. 1989. *Managing Money in Higher Education*. San Francisco: Jossey-Bass.

Warner, T.R. 1988. "College Costs: A View From a Private University." *College Board Review* 147: 16-19+.

Weiss, S. September 26, 1990. "Pressed on Budget, CUNY Turns Away Students." *New York Times*. B6.

Wilson, R. 1987. "Critics Tell House Panel That Colleges Waste Money on Overpaid Professors and Duplicate Programs." *Chronicle of Higher Education*. A1+.

———. February 21, 1990. "Only 15 Percent of Students Graduate in 4 Years, A New Study Finds." *Chronicle of Higher Education* 36: A1+.

Witmer, D.R. Winter 1972. "Cost Studies in Higher Education." *Review of Educational Research* 42: 99-127.

Wittstruck, J.R. 1988. *Challenges and Opportunities: Minorities in Missouri Higher Education*. Jefferson City: Missouri Coordinating Board for Higher Education. ED 310 821. 57 pp. MF–01; PC–03.

Wittstruck, J.R., and S.M. Bragg. 1988. *Focus on Price Trends in Public Higher Education*. Denver, Colo.: State Higher Education Executive Officers. ED 299 879. 123 pp. MF–01; PC–05.

Yuker, H.E. 1984. *Faculty Workload: Research, Theory, and Interpretation*. ASHE-ERIC Higher Education Research Report No. 10. Washington, D.C.: ERIC Clearinghouse on Higher Education. ED 259 691. 120 pp. MF–01; PC–05.

Zemsky, R., and W.F. Massy. November/December 1990. "Cost Containment: Committing to a New Economic Reality." *Change*. 16-22.

INDEX

A

Adjunct faculty, 42
Administrative costs
    colleges and universities, 40
    control of, 69
    higher education, 3
Administrative salaries
    colleges and universities, 41
Administrators, return to faculty, 70
Agriculture Department, 22
Albright College, 47
Alexander, Lamar, 21
Amenities
    colleges and universities, 15
American Association of State Colleges and Universities, 27
American Association of Universities, 13
    report, 58
American Association of University Professors, 69
Appropriation cuts, higher education, 1

B

Baldwin-Wallace College, 47
Beloit College, 47
Benefit expenditures, 48
Bennett, William, 20
Break-even analysis, 75
Budget reductions, colleges and universities, 83
Budgeting, 2

C

California state university system, 44
Cambridge, 39
Carnegie Committee on Higher Education, 11
Classes
    full-time, 73
    part-time, 73
College operations
    efficiency, 6
College work-study programs, 28
Colleges and universities
    external funds, 13
    financial difficulty, 7
    financial officers, 5
    social purposes, 12
Community college funding
    Florida, 14
Congressional Budget Office, 24
Consensus management, 40

New York, City University of, 86
Nonprofit organizations, 12

O
Ohio State University
supercomputer network, 67
Online databases, 54
Overeducation
United States, 14

P
Part-time faculty, 73
Payments in lieu of taxes
colleges and universities, 39
Peace dividend, 24
Pell grants, 21, 28
Pension funds
colleges and universities, 62]
Perkins loans, 28
Pittsburgh, 39
Position reduction
colleges and universities, 87
Princeton University, 20
Private giving
colleges and universities, 31
Productivity
faculty, 49
ProfScam, 50
Programs, 74
costs, 11
quality, 69
revenues, 76
reviews, 76
self-supporting, 75
termination, 89
Project funding, 24
Public colleges
closure, 27
funding, 27

R
Ratchet effect
administrative staff, 41
Reallocation of resources, 8, 11
Recruiting expenses, 3
Research
cost reimbursement, 59
state funding, 30

ASHE-ERIC HIGHER EDUCATION REPORTS

Since 1983, the Association for the Study of Higher Education (ASHE) and the Educational Resources Information Center (ERIC) Clearinghouse on Higher Education, a sponsored project of the School of Education and Human Development at The George Washington University, have cosponsored the *ASHE-ERIC Higher Education Report* series. The 1991 series is the twentieth overall and the third to be published by the School of Education and Human Development at the George Washington University.

Each monograph is the definitive analysis of a tough higher education problem, based on thorough research of pertinent literature and institutional experiences. Topics are identified by a national survey. Noted practitioners and scholars are then commissioned to write the reports, with experts providing critical reviews of each manuscript before publication.

Eight monographs (10 before 1985) in the ASHE-ERIC Higher Education Report series are published each year and are available on individual and subscription bases. Subscription to eight issues is $90.00 annually; $70 to members of AAHE, AIR, or AERA; and $60 to ASHE members. All foreign subscribers must include an additional $10 per series year for postage.

To order single copies of existing reports, use the order form on the last page of this book. Regular prices, and special rates available to members of AAHE, AIR, AERA and ASHE, are as follows:

Series	Regular	Members
1990 and 91	$17.00	$12.75
1988 and 89	15.00	11.25
1985 to 87	10.00	7.50
1983 and 84	7.50	6.00
before 1983	6.50	5.00

Price includes book rate postage within the U.S. For foreign orders, please add $1.00 per book. Fast United Parcel Service available within the contiguous U.S. at $2.50 for each order under $50.00, and calculated at 5% of invoice total for orders $50.00 or above.

All orders under $45.00 must be prepaid. Make check payable to ASHE-ERIC. For Visa or MasterCard, include card number, expiration date and signature. A bulk discount of 10% is available on orders of 10 or more books, and 40% on orders of 25 or more books (not applicable on subscriptions).

Address order to
ASHE-ERIC Higher Education Reports
The George Washington University
1 Dupont Circle, Suite 630
Washington, DC 20036
Or phone (202) 296-2597
Write or call for a complete catalog.

1991 ASHE-ERIC Higher Education Reports

1. Active Learning: Creating Excitement in the Classroom
   Charles C. Bonwell and James A. Eison

2. Realizing Gender Equality in Higher Education: The Need to Integrate Work/Family Issues
   Nancy Hensel

3. Academic Advising for Student Success: A System of Shared Responsibility
   by Susan H. Frost

4. Cooperative Learning: Increasing College Faculty Instructional Productivity
   by David W. Johnson, Roger T. Johnson, and Karl A. Smith

5. High School–College Partnerships: Conceptual Models, Programs, and Issues
   by Arthur Richard Greenberg

6. Meeting the Mandate: Renewing the College and Departmental Curriculum
   by William Toombs and William Tierney

7. Faculty Collaboration: Enhancing the Quality of Scholarship and Teaching
   by Ann E. Austin and Roger G. Baldwin

1990 ASHE-ERIC Higher Education Reports

1. The Campus Green: Fund Raising in Higher Education
   Barbara E. Brittingham and Thomas R. Pezzullo

2. The Emeritus Professor: Old Rank - New Meaning
   James E. Mauch, Jack W. Birch, and Jack Matthews

3. "High Risk" Students in Higher Education: Future Trends
   Dionne J. Jones and Betty Collier Watson

4. Budgeting for Higher Education at the State Level: Enigma, Paradox, and Ritual
   Daniel T. Layzell and Jan W. Lyddon

5. Proprietary Schools: Programs, Policies, and Prospects
   John B. Lee and Jamie P. Merisotis

6. College Choice: Understanding Student Enrollment Behavior
   Michael B. Paulsen

7. Pursuing Diversity: Recruiting College Minority Students
   Barbara Astone and Elsa Nuñez-Wormack

8. Social Consciousness and Career Awareness: Emerging Link in Higher Education
   John S. Swift, Jr.

1989 ASHE-ERIC Higher Education Reports

1. Making Sense of Administrative Leadership: The 'L' Word in Higher Education
   Estela M. Bensimon, Anna Neumann, and Robert Birnbaum

2. Affirmative Rhetoric, Negative Action: African-American and Hispanic Faculty at Predominantly White Universities
   Valora Washington and William Harvey

3. Postsecondary Developmental Programs: A Traditional Agenda with New Imperatives
   Louise M. Tomlinson

4. The Old College Try: Balancing Athletics and Academics in Higher Education
   John R. Thelin and Lawrence L. Wiseman

5. The Challenge of Diversity: Involvement or Alienation in the Academy?
   Daryl G. Smith

6. Student Goals for College and Courses: A Missing Link in Assessing and Improving Academic Achievement
   Joan S. Stark, Kathleen M. Shaw, and Malcolm A. Lowther

7. The Student as Commuter: Developing a Comprehensive Institutional Response
   Barbara Jacoby

8. Renewing Civic Capacity: Preparing College Students for Service and Citizenship
   Suzanne W. Morse

1988 ASHE-ERIC Higher Education Reports

1. The Invisible Tapestry: Culture in American Colleges and Universities
   George D. Kuh and Elizabeth J. Whitt

2. Critical Thinking: Theory, Research, Practice, and Possibilities
   Joanne Gainen Kurfiss

3. Developing Academic Programs: The Climate for Innovation
   Daniel T. Seymour

4. Peer Teaching: To Teach is To Learn Twice
   Neal A. Whitman

5. Higher Education and State Governments: Renewed Partnership, Cooperation, or Competition?
   Edward R. Hines

6. Entrepreneurship and Higher Education: Lessons for Colleges, Universities, and Industry
   James S. Fairweather

7. Planning for Microcomputers in Higher Education: Strategies for the Next Generation
   Reynolds Ferrante, John Hayman, Mary Susan Carlson, and Harry Phillips

8. The Challenge for Research in Higher Education: Harmonizing Excellence and Utility
   Alan W. Lindsay and Ruth T. Neumann

1987 ASHE-ERIC Higher Education Reports

1. Incentive Early Retirement Programs for Faculty: Innovative Responses to a Changing Environment
   Jay L. Chronister and Thomas R. Kepple, Jr.

2. Working Effectively with Trustees: Building Cooperative Campus Leadership
   Barbara E. Taylor

3. Formal Recognition of Employer-Sponsored Instruction: Conflict and Collegiality in Postsecondary Education
   Nancy S. Nash and Elizabeth M. Hawthorne

4. Learning Styles: Implications for Improving Educational Practices
   Charles S. Claxton and Patricia H. Murrell

5. Higher Education Leadership: Enhancing Skills through Professional Development Programs
   Sharon A. McDade

6. Higher Education and the Public Trust: Improving Stature in Colleges and Universities
   Richard L. Alfred and Julie Weissman

7. College Student Outcomes Assessment: A Talent Development Perspective
   Maryann Jacobi, Alexander Astin, and Frank Ayala, Jr.

8. Opportunity from Strength: Strategic Planning Clarified with Case Examples
   Robert G. Cope

1986 ASHE-ERIC Higher Education Reports

1. Post-tenure Faculty Evaluation: Threat or Opportunity?
   Christine M. Licata

2. Blue Ribbon Commissions and Higher Education: Changing Academe from the Outside
   Janet R. Johnson and Laurence R. Marcus

3. Responsive Professional Education: Balancing Outcomes and Opportunities
   Joan S. Stark, Malcolm A. Lowther, and Bonnie M.K. Hagerty

4. Increasing Students' Learning: A Faculty Guide to Reducing Stress among Students
   Neal A. Whitman, David C. Spendlove, and Claire H. Clark

5. Student Financial Aid and Women: Equity Dilemma?
   Mary Moran

6. The Master's Degree: Tradition, Diversity, Innovation
   Judith S. Glazer

7. The College, the Constitution, and the Consumer Student: Implications for Policy and Practice
   Robert M. Hendrickson and Annette Gibbs

8. Selecting College and University Personnel: The Quest and the Question
   Richard A. Kaplowitz

1985 ASHE-ERIC Higher Education Reports

1. Flexibility in Academic Staffing: Effective Policies and Practices
   Kenneth P. Mortimer, Marque Bagshaw, and Andrew T. Masland

2. Associations in Action: The Washington, D.C. Higher Education Community
   Harland G. Bloland

3. And on the Seventh Day: Faculty Consulting and Supplemental Income
   Carol M. Boyer and Darrell R. Lewis

4. Faculty Research Performance: Lessons from the Sciences and Social Sciences
   John W. Creswell

5. Academic Program Review: Institutional Approaches, Expectations, and Controversies
   Clifton F. Conrad and Richard F. Wilson

6. Students in Urban Settings: Achieving the Baccalaureate Degree
   Richard C. Richardson, Jr. and Louis W. Bender

7. Serving More Than Students: A Critical Need for College Student Personnel Services
   Peter H. Garland

8. Faculty Participation in Decision Making: Necessity or Luxury?
   Carol E. Floyd

1984 ASHE-ERIC Higher Education Reports

1. Adult Learning: State Policies and Institutional Practices
   K. Patricia Cross and Anne-Marie McCartan

2. Student Stress: Effects and Solutions
   Neal A. Whitman, David C. Spendlove, and Claire H. Clark

3. Part-time Faulty: Higher Education at a Crossroads
   Judith M. Gappa

4. Sex Discrimination Law in Higher Education: The Lessons of
   the Past Decade. ED 252 169.*
   J. Ralph Lindgren, Patti T. Ota, Perry A. Zirkel, and Nan Van Gieson

5. Faculty Freedoms and Institutional Accountability: Interactions
   and Conflicts
   Steven G. Olswang and Barbara A. Lee

6. The High Technology Connection: Academic/Industrial Cooperation for Economic Growth
   Lynn G. Johnson

7. Employee Educational Programs: Implications for Industry and
   Higher Education. ED 258 501.*
   Suzanne W. Morse

8. Academic Libraries: The Changing Knowledge Centers of Colleges and Universities
   Barbara B. Moran

9. Futures Research and the Strategic Planning Process: Implications for Higher Education
   James L. Morrison, William L. Renfro, and Wayne I. Boucher

10. Faculty Workload: Research, Theory, and Interpretation
    Harold E. Yuker

*Out-of-print. Available through EDRS. Call 1-800-443-ERIC.

ORDER FORM

Quantity   **Amount**

_____ Please begin my subscription to the 1991 *ASHE-ERIC Higher Education Reports* at $90.00, 33% off the cover price, starting with Report 1, 1991.   _____

_____ Please send a complete set of the 1990 *ASHE-ERIC Higher Education Reports* at $80.00, 41% off the cover price.   _____

_____ Outside the U.S., add $10.00 per series for postage.   _____

Individual reports are avilable at the following prices:

1990 and 1991, $17.00	1983 and 1984, $7.50
1988 and 1989, $15.00	1982 and back, $6.50
1985 to 1987, $10.00	

Book rate postage within the U.S. is included. Outside U.S., please add $1.00 per book for postage. Fast U.P.S. shipping is available within the contiguous U.S. at $2.50 for each order under $50.00, and calculated at 5% of invoice total for orders $50.00 or above. All orders under $45.00 must be prepaid.

PLEASE SEND ME THE FOLLOWING REPORTS:

Quantity	Report No.	Year	Title	Amount

Subtotal:	
Foreign or UPS:	
Total Due:	

Please check one of the following:
- ☐ Check enclosed, payable to GWU-ERIC.
- ☐ Purchase order attached ($45.00 minimum).
- ☐ Charge my credit card indicated below:
    - ☐ Visa   ☐ MasterCard

Expiration Date _____

Name _____

Title _____

Institution _____

Address _____

City _____ State _____ Zip _____

Phone _____

Signature _____ Date _____

SEND ALL ORDERS TO:
ASHE-ERIC Higher Education Reports
The George Washington University
One Dupont Circle, Suite 630
Washington, DC 20036-1183
Phone: (202) 296-2597

Quantity   **Amount**

_____ Please begin my subscription to the 1991 *ASHE-ERIC Higher Education Reports* at $90.00, 33% off the cover price, starting with Report 1, 1991.   _____

_____ Please send a complete set of the 1990 *ASHE-ERIC Higher Education Reports* at $80.00, 41% off the cover price.   _____

_____ Outside the U.S., add $10.00 per series for postage.   _____

Individual reports are avilable at the following prices:

1990 and 1991, $17.00	1983 and 1984, $7.50
1988 and 1989, $15.00	1982 and back, $6.50
1985 to 1987, $10.00	

Book rate postage within the U.S. is included. Outside U.S., please add $1.00 per book for postage. Fast U.P.S. shipping is available within the contiguous U.S. at $2.50 for each order under $50.00, and calculated at 5% of invoice total for orders $50.00 or above. All orders under $45.00 must be prepaid.

PLEASE SEND ME THE FOLLOWING REPORTS:

Quantity	Report No.	Year	Title	Amount

Subtotal:	
Foreign or UPS:	
Total Due:	

Please check one of the following:

☐ Check enclosed, payable to GWU–ERIC.
☐ Purchase order attached ($45.00 minimum).
☐ Charge my credit card indicated below:
   ☐ Visa   ☐ MasterCard

☐☐☐☐☐☐☐☐☐☐☐☐☐☐☐☐☐☐☐

Expiration Date _____

Name _____

Title _____

Institution _____

Address _____

City _____ State _____ Zip _____

Phone _____

Signature _____ Date _____

SEND ALL ORDERS TO:
ASHE-ERIC Higher Education Reports
The George Washington University
One Dupont Circle, Suite 630
Washington, DC 20036-1183
Phone: (202) 296-2597